The Encyclopedia Of
Icebreakers

Structured Activities That Warm-Up, Motivate, Challenge, Acquaint and Energize

Sue Forbess-Greene, L.M.S.W.

Applied Skills Press
8517 Production Avenue
P.O. Box 26240
San Diego, CA 92126

Contents

Feedback and Disclosure continued

Games and Brainteasers   **133**

Openers and Warm-ups continued

Professional Development Topics 337

Professional Development Topics continued

Trainer's Introduction

The Encyclopedia of Icebreakers is the first comprehensive listing of introductory activities designed to make learning easier for the participants involved in workshops, courses, conferences, and skill-development training programs. Icebreakers are tools that enable the group leader to foster interaction, stimulate creative thinking, challenge basic assumptions, illustrate new concepts, and introduce specific material. The activities are appropriate for use in business, industry, education, health care, and other human service settings. Almost all of the icebreakers in this reference text require less than 30 minutes, demand little, if any, advance preparation, are simple to implement, and are flexible enough to be used with an unlimited range of topics. The group leader's careful selection and execution of these structured activities will help ensure that the participants are receptive to the information and/or skills presented during the learning program.

Organization of Icebreakers

All icebreakers are not the same. Thus, the primary goal, level of impact, and degree of intensity will vary significantly among the activities. *The Encyclopedia of Icebreakers* contains six divisions: Energizers and Tension Reducers, Feedback and Disclosure, Games and Brainteasers, Getting Acquainted, Openers and Warm-Ups, and Professional Development Topics. Each division contains structured activities that vary slightly in time requirement, optimum number of participants, space requirement, and material(s) needed. The divisions will expedite the group leader's ability to choose those icebreakers that most effectively meet his or her needs as well as the needs of the group members.

Occasionally the group leader will encounter an icebreaker that could, in theory, be listed in more than one division. For example, an activity placed in the Getting Acquainted division may also be appropriate to the Feedback and Disclosure division. Because of this potential overlapping, the icebreakers have been grouped according to *primary* function. The introductory page to each division indicates the specific purpose of, and rationale for, the activities that follow.

Icebreaker Format

Each icebreaker, regardless of the division under which it has been listed, uses the same outline headings: Activity Summary, Training Application, Trainer Administration, Variation(s), and Trainer's Notes. This easy-to-use cookbook format allows the group leader to glance at an icebreaker and quickly determine its applicability for his or her specific purpose. In addition, the outline format provides step-by-step instructions that simplify the use of each icebreaker. Specifically, the headings used in the format address the following:

Activity Summary contains a one or two sentence synopsis of the icebreaker and a general recommendation for when, during the group's development, its use is most appropriate.

Training Application provides specific information on the amount of time the activity requires, the optimum size of the group, the particular space required, and, when necessary, the materials needed for the activity.

Trainer Administration gives step-by-step instructions on how to implement the activity. Before conducting the icebreaker, the group leader must, of course, take into account his or her specific needs and conditions.

Variation(s) suggests possible modifications of the basic activity that will provide additional flexibility for the group leader. Additional variations that more effectively meet the needs of the specific program are encouraged.

Trainer's Notes allows the group leader enough space to record, for future reference, his or her comments about the icebreaker, i.e., its general effectiveness, additional uses, possible modifications, etc.

Within a division each icebreaker is arranged alphabetically by its title. A number of the icebreakers contain lists or materials that are referenced in the Training Application and Trainer Administration sections. These lists or materials are typically intended as handouts for the participants; therefore, to facilitate duplication, they are presented on separate pages at the end of the respective activities.

The Effective Use of Icebreakers

By their very nature, icebreakers help create an atmosphere that reduces the participants' inhibitions and increases their awareness. However, the group leader must keep in mind that any structured activity can be misused. To minimize the risks and maximize the benefits of using icebreakers, the leader should keep in mind the following guidelines.

1. Group members should never be forced to participate in an acitivity. Although the group leader may encourage total participation, each learner must understand that he or she has the right to refrain from engaging in any icebreaker that appears too uncomfortable or awkward.

2. Unless otherwise agreed, the information generated during an activity should be considered confidential. In particular, the Getting Acquainted and Feedback and Disclosure divisions, which contain icebreakers that may solicit personal information, should be treated with care.

3. The group leader serves as an important role model for the participants. The group leader will find that his or her active participation in an icebreaker may help reduce some of the participants' initial inhibitions and thus promote moderate risk taking.

4. Before implementing any activity, the group leader needs to consider carefully its appropriateness. The overuse or premature use of an icebreaker can lead to group members' feeling that the structure is too contrived or manipulative. The leader needs to keep in mind that an icebreaker is simply a learning tool, not an end in and of itself.

5. Although icebreakers, unlike some other forms of structured activities, do not require formal debriefing, the group leader should maintain an acute awareness of the development of the participants and of the group itself. Issues regarding disclosure, cohesiveness, trust, team building, risk taking, control, and dependence should be monitored continuously.

These general guidelines will help the group leader make the most out of the material contained in this encyclopedia. When used with sensitivity to individual and group needs, these icebreakers can be unusually flexible and potent aids for learning.

Bridging the Gap

One of the most important keys to the successful use of icebreakers is the group leader's ability to bridge the gap between the activity and the material that follows. Because most icebreakers are not topic oriented (except those in the professional-development topics division), smooth transitions are crucial. If, for example, in a workshop on supervision a group leader uses an icebreaker that challenges the participants to brainstorm the creative uses of old refrigerators, he or she may lead into content material by underscoring how useful creative thinking can be to someone who manages others. Each icebreaker, regardless of its division, requires that the group leader use his or her resourcefulness in making the transition of focus. Indeed, some icebreakers lend themselves more easily to content shifts than others. Yet if the trainer chooses an icebreaker wisely, he or she will have little difficulty in making a transition between the experiential activity and the topic-based information that follows.

The surface nature of icebreakers allows the group leader to proceed without lengthy debriefing or processing. However, if an activity does generate notable reactions, whether they be thoughts or feelings, the leader must assume primary responsibility for tying loose ends or clarifying issues. Although this situation will occur rarely, a ready posture will make for a more productive transition and avoid potentially disruptive encounters with group members who may have unresolved or conflicting emotions about the experience.

Icebreaker Divisions

As noted previously, *The Encyclopedia or Icebreakers* contains six divisions, the grouping of icebreakers being based upon the primary purpose of each structured experience. Specifically, the divisions are centered around the following areas.

Energizers and Tension Reducers. The Energizers and Tension Reducers division contains icebreakers that shift the emotional nature of the group. Most effectively used when the participants appear "flat" or overly anxious, these activities serve as catalysts for energizing or for reducing tension. Some of the energizers require mild physical contact.

Feedback and Disclosure. The Feedback and Disclosure division contains icebreakers that are aimed at establishing interactions of a personal nature. Going beyond mere introductions, these activities often explore thoughts, feelings, perceptions, impressions, and reactions. Cautious selection is advised for use in groups that are not directed toward personal exploration.

Games and Brainteasers. The Games and Brainteasers division contains icebreakers that stimulate creative thinking, alternative perceptions, and the examination of basic assumptions. These activities often facilitate a competitive environment by pitting individuals or teams against one another.

Getting Acquainted. The Getting Acquainted division contains icebreakers that provide the group members with opportunities to learn more about one another in a nonthreatening manner. These activities generally solicit only surface information, i.e., work responsibilities, general goals and values, enjoyable fantasies, etc. Getting-acquainted icebreakers are ideal for quickly mixing the group and for lowering barriers.

Professional Development Topics. The Professional Development Topics division contains icebreakers that are related to specific professional subjects. Exploring such topics as leadership, supervision, team building, assessment, motivation, and problem solving, these activities provide an obvious lead-in to content-based material. Since the term "professional development" is used in a broad sense, the icebreakers are applicable to almost any work setting.

The six divisions offer the group leader a variety of icebreakers that can meet his or her needs for almost any situation. Furthermore, the group leader will find that the creative modification of any given icebreaker will simply expand its use as well as increase the impact of its initial purpose.

Summary

Learning is a process that, in its most effective form, is both broadening and enjoyable. *The Encyclopedia of Icebreakers* offers the group leader a vast resource of learning tools that, when used appropriately, can heighten the effectiveness of any educational event. This professional text provides a variety of designs that can help ensure that a workshop, course, or program is successful, because the materials contained in this encyclopedia will, indeed, warm-up, motivate, challenge, acquaint, and energize participants.

Energizers and Tension Reducers

The icebreakers in this division are designed to reduce the anxiety level of the group members and/or to increase the degree of group energy. Commonly used when the participants appear overly stressed or when the group seems "flat," energizers and tension reducers shift the emotional atmosphere of the learning environment. The group leader's ability to influence the mood of the group is of great value when he or she is attempting to introduce information that is best received under specific conditions. For example, if the group leader is planning to conduct a session that requires a discussion format, an energizer or tension reducer can help set the stage for increased interaction. Once group members have experienced an icebreaker that helps them shed their inhibitions or reduce the stresses they may be experiencing, they are more likely to be receptive to a less guarded dialogue about the information, issues, skills, etc., that are to be introduced.

Some of the icebreakers in this division require some degree of physical contact between participants. Since any form of physical contact can be perceived as threatening, the group leader should exercise caution in selecting an activity. Most groups, however, will readily accept mild physical contact if the proper learning environment has been established. The group leader should, of course, honor the feelings of any participant who finds taking part in a specific activity too uncomfortable or awkward.

The group leader's behavior will generally serve as a model for his or her participants. If the leader approaches a selected energizer or tension reducer with sensitivity and a sense of adventure, he or she will do much to increase the likelihood that the icebreaker will be effective. When selected appropriately and executed properly, the following activities can make most learning events more enjoyable and exciting.

Barnyard

This exercise asks the participants to use animal noises to disguise their identities. Since the participants need to be familiar with one another and know one another's names, this activity is generally more effective when used during the later stage of the training program or session.

Time Reference: Approximately 10 to 15 minutes.
Group Size: Best suited for a group of 10 to 20 participants.
Space Required: An unobstructed area without tables or chairs.
Materials Needed: A large handkerchief or scarf to serve as a blindfold.

1. The trainer asks the group members to stand and form a large circle.
2. When the participants are in position, the group leader explains that this game requires them to disguise their identities by imitating the sounds of animals.
3. The trainer solicits a volunteer to stand in the middle of the circle and serve as the "farmer." The group leader then blindfolds the farmer and twirls him or her around so that he or she is disoriented.
4. The farmer then calls out the name of an animal that might be found on a farm. For example: cow, chicken, horse, duck, pig, etc. The participant standing in front of, or closest to, the farmer must then imitate the sound that is appropriate for the animal. For example: If the farmer calls out "cow," the participant must moo.
5. The farmer's task is to guess the person's true identity. If the farmer wishes, he or she may ask the participant to repeat the sound two times. The farmer may make only one guess.
6. If the farmer guesses the participant's identity incorrectly, he or she is twirled around again and must call out a new animal for another participant to imitate. This procedure continues until the farmer has guessed some group member's identity.

7. When the farmer has guessed a participant's identity correctly, that participant becomes the blindfolded farmer, and the original farmer joins the group members in the circle.
8. The game continues for 10 minutes or until all of the participants have had an opportunity to assume the role of the farmer.

Variations
■ The group leader may instruct all of the participants to imitate the sound of the animal the farmer calls out. The farmer must then try to sort the sounds and guess the identity of the participant standing in front of, or closest to, him or her.

■ If the group contains more than 20 participants, the trainer may have two or more farmers take part in the exercise at the same time.

Trainer's Notes

_____

_____

_____

_____

_____

_____

_____

_____

Bunny Hop

This exercise energizes the participants as they perform a well-known dance, the Bunny Hop. This activity is generally more effective when used during the later stage of the training program or session.

**Training
Application**

Time Reference: Approximately 5 to 10 minutes.

Group Size: Best suited for a group of 20 or fewer participants. If the group contains more than 20 participants, two subgroups should be formed.

Space Required: An unobstructed area without tables or chairs. The room must be large enough to permit the unrestricted movement of the learners.

Materials Needed: For the trainer, the Bunny Hop to Music Sheet (see the last page of this exercise).

**Trainer
Administration**

1. The trainer explains that the participants will be using a well-known dance, the Bunny Hop, as an energizer.
2. The group leader then solicits a volunteer to lead the dance. The participants are asked to form one line, with each of the group members holding on to the waist of the person standing in front of him or her.
3. The trainer then asks the group members to practice singing "The Farmer in the Dell." As they practice, the trainer demonstrates the Bunny Hop, showing how the steps of the dance correspond to the phrases in the song (see the Bunny Hop to Music Sheet). The trainer then tells the group to practice singing and dancing at the same time.
4. After a brief practice, the volunteer-leader begins the singing and dancing. (The trainer tells the leader to speed up or slow down the pace as necessary to provide variety to the exercise.)
5. The volunteer then leads the group around the room as they repeat the song and the dance steps at least five times.

Variations

■ The trainer may ask the participants to do the Bunny Hop without music.

■ In the middle of the dance, the group leader may ask the participants to reverse the line so that the person who was last is now the leader of the dance.

■ The trainer may use other music or songs that fit the rhythm of the dance. For example: "Row, Row, Row Your Boat," "Yankee Doodle," "The Bunny Hop," etc.

Trainer's Notes

_____

_____

_____

_____

_____

_____

_____

_____

BUNNY HOP TO MUSIC SHEET

"The farmer in the dell" (kick right foot to the right two times, touching heel to floor with each kick)

"The farmer in the dell" (kick left foot to the left two times, touching heel to floor with each kick)

"Hi ho" (hop one step forward with both feet together)

"The dairy-o" (hop one step backward with both feet together)

"The farmer in the dell" (hop forward three times with both feet together)

Card Relay

Activity Summary   This exercise asks the participants, working in teams, to pass playing cards quickly to their fellow team members. This icebreaker is effective at any time during the training program.

Training Application

Time Reference: Approximately 5 to 10 minutes.
Group Size: Best suited for a group of 10 to 20 participants.
Space Required: A room that has the potential for flexible seating.
Materials Needed: Two decks of playing cards.

Trainer Administration

1. The trainer begins by dividing the group members into two teams, with an equal number of participants on each team. If the group contains an uneven number, one participant can serve as a referee, or the trainer can play on one of the teams.
2. When the two teams have formed, the group leader asks them to position their chairs in two parallel rows so that the teams sit facing one another.
3. After the teams are seated, the trainer tells them that they will be competing in a relay in which they pass playing cards down their respective rows.
4. After giving the first person in each row a deck of cards, the trainer explains the rules of the game.
   a. At a signal, the first player in each row takes a card from the top of the deck and hands it to the team member sitting next to him or her.
   b. This person grasps the card in the hand closest to the team row leader, transfers the card to the other hand, and passes it to the next person down the row. As the person passes one card, he or she reaches out the other hand to get the next card from the line leader.
   c. In this manner each person receives and passes cards down his or her team's row.
   d. When the last person in each row receives a card, he or she drops it to the floor next to his or her chair.
   e. If, in receiving or passing, a player drops a card, he or she must retrieve and pass that

card before accepting another card from the person preceding him or her in the line.

   f. The winner will be the team that finishes first and can collect and count 52 passed cards.

5. After explaining the rules, the trainer may allow the teams several minutes in which to practice passing two cards down the rows.

6. The group leader then gives a signal, and the relay begins.

Variations

■ The group leader may ask both teams to play with every other one of their team members wearing blindfolds.

■ The trainer may ask the last person in each team's row to pick the cards off the floor and pass them quickly, one at a time, back up the row. The winner is the team that can pass its cards more quickly down the row and then back to the line leader, who collects and counts the cards.

Trainer's Notes

_____

_____

_____

_____

_____

_____

_____

_____

Caterpillar Race

Activity Summary

This exercise reduces the participants' inhibitions as they form human caterpillars and compete in an unusual race. This icebreaker is effective at any time during the learning program.

Training Application

Time Reference: Approximately 5 to 10 minutes.

Group Size: Unlimited, but best suited for a group of 12 or more participants.

Space Required: An unobstructed area without tables or chairs.

Materials Needed: None.

Trainer Administration

1. The trainer begins the exercise by asking the participants to divide into two groups, or teams, with an equal number of group members on each team.

2. When the teams have formed, the group leader explains that the teams will be racing against one another and, if necessary, asks the participants to clear the room of all obstacles.

3. After instructing each team to line up behind an imaginary starting line, the trainer places one chair for each team approximately 30 feet away from the line.

4. The group leader then tells the participants that each team is to form a human caterpillar as its members hold on to the waists of the persons standing in front of them.

5. The trainer explains that the object of the game is for the human caterpillars to move across the room, around the chair, and back to the starting line without any team member losing hold of the waist of the person in front of him or her. If a team member does lose his or her grip, that team's human caterpillar must return to the starting line and begin again.

6. The group leader gives a signal, and the race begins.

7. The human caterpillar that is the first to complete the course without losing any members is declared the winner.

Variations

■ The trainer may instruct the human caterpillars to walk backwards around the course, following the game rules established in step #5 of the Trainer Administration section.

■ The group leader may ask the team members to form their caterpillars by placing their hands on the shoulders, instead of the waists, of the persons in front of them.

■ The trainer may explain that the caterpillar is to add a piece to its body each time it completes the race course. In this variation, the chairs are positioned approximately 20 feet in front of the starting line. At a signal from the trainer, the player in the front of each team's line walks out around the chair and then back to the starting line. When the player returns to the starting line, the next person in line grabs the first player's waist and they traverse the course. The third person in line joins the other two, and so on until all of the team members have finished their human caterpillar and then completed the course.

Trainer's Notes

_____

_____

_____

_____

_____

_____

_____

Creative Contraptions

Activity
Summary This exercise stimulates the participants' creativity by having them act out machines while the other group members attempt to guess the object's identity and its functions. This activity is generally more effective when used during the later stage of the training program or session.

Training
Application *Time Reference:* Approximately 20 to 25 minutes.

Group Size: Unlimited, but best suited for a group of 15 to 25 participants.

Space Required: A large, unobstructed area without tables or chairs. Several small meeting rooms or areas that allow for private or semi-private interaction are also needed.

Materials Needed: For the trainer, the Sample Machines List (see the last page of this exercise).

Trainer
Administration 1. The trainer tells the group members that they will be participating in an exercise that requires teamwork.

2. Next the group leader explains that the participants will be divided into work groups. Each group will be given 10 minutes in which to form a human machine using all of the members of their particular group to represent parts of the machine. Each work group's human machine must insofar as possible resemble the machine the group has been asked to depict. Furthermore, all of the groups will be asked to demonstrate their machines for the entire group.

3. After dividing the participants into three or four separate work groups, the trainer gives each group a slip of paper that describes the machine they are to become (see Sample Machines List). Since this exercise involves some degree of secrecy, the work groups are to locate areas in which they can work privately.

4. After 10 minutes the trainer calls all of the work groups back into the room and then chooses a group to give the first demonstration. When the work group members have formed their "creative contraption," the other participants attempt to guess the machine and its product.

5. The exercise continues until all of the work groups have demonstrated their machines.

Variations
■ The trainer may ask that each work group choose the machine that its members wish to demonstrate.
■ The group leader may suggest that each work group have the various parts of its machine imitate their particular sounds.
■ The trainer may give all of the groups the same kind of machinery to design.
■ The group leader may have the entire group create one machine.

Trainer's Notes

_____

_____

_____

_____

_____

_____

_____

_____

SAMPLE MACHINES LIST

1. Donut-hole-punching machine
2. Bottle-capping machine
3. Cigarette-making machine
4. Book-binding machine
5. Hotdog-roll-making machine
6. Toaster
7. Gasoline pump
8. Riding lawn mower
9. Milkshake-making machine
10. Computerized scoreboard

Creative Dough

This exercise asks the participants to create items from imaginary dough. This activity is generally more effective when used during the later stage of the training program or session.

Time Reference: Approximately 10 to 15 minutes.
Group Size: Unlimited.
Space Required: An unobstructed area without tables or chairs. The room must be large enough to permit the unrestricted movement of the learners.
Materials Needed: None.

1. The group leader first asks the participants to stand and form a circle.
2. When the group members are in position, the trainer explains that in the center of the circle is an imaginary ball of dough. The participants will be using the dough to sculpt some objects that are used frequently. For example: a chair, a bicycle, a telephone, a broom, etc.
3. Next the group leader solicits a volunteer to walk to the center of the circle, take as much of the dough as he or she needs, and then sculpt some common object.
4. The rest of the participants watch closely and spontaneously call out their guesses as to the identity of the item that the volunteer is making.
5. The person who guesses correctly then moves into the circle and fashions an object from the imaginary dough, while the other group members attempt to guess the item's identity.
6. If, after two minutes, the group members cannot guess the item being sculpted or, if necessary, resculpted, the volunteer identifies the object. He or she then returns to the circle, and a new volunteer comes forward to make an item from the imaginary dough.
7. The game continues for 5 to 10 minutes, with each person who guesses an object correctly then receiving an opportunity to make an item from the imaginary dough.

Variations ■ The trainer may request that the group members sculpt edible objects. For example: a banana, a cake, a pie, a stew, etc.

■ The group leader may ask the participants to fashion objects that are in the room.

■ If the group is large, the trainer may direct two or three participants to move into the circle and simultaneously create objects. When one object is guessed by an observing group member, the participant returns to the outer circle, and the person who guessed the object's identity comes forward to make an item from the imaginary dough.

Trainer's Notes _____

_____

_____

_____

_____

_____

_____

_____

Extraterrestrial Journey

Activity Summary

This exercise asks the participants to fantasize a journey into outer space. This activity is generally more effective when used during the later stage of the training program or session.

Training Application

Time Reference: Approximately 10 to 15 minutes.
Group Size: Unlimited.
Space Required: An unobstructed area without tables or chairs.
Materials Needed: For the trainer, the Extraterrestrial Journey Sheet (see the last page of this exercise).

Trainer Administration

1. The trainer begins the exercise by telling the participants that they are going to take a journey into outer space.
2. The group members are either to sit comfortably in their chairs or to lie in relaxed positions on the floor.
3. The lights are then dimmed. The trainer asks the participants to close their eyes and to let all of their present thoughts, problems, etc. float out of their minds.
4. After asking the group members to concentrate and attempt to visualize the scene, the trainer begins a structured fantasy journey through space. [The story (see Extraterrestrial Journey Sheet) is to be used as a base of reference in guiding the participants into the fantasy. The story should be read slowly and calmly with appropriate pauses used to indicate changes in scene and mood. The trainer can add details to or vary slightly the content of the story.]
5. When the journey is over, the trainer "debriefs" the group members, asking them to share their feelings about the special journey they have just completed.

Variations

■ The trainer asks the participants to sit quietly and create their own individual fantasies. For example: a trip up the Amazon River, a solitary journey down into Carlsbad Caverns, an experience as a soloist with the New York City Ballet, etc.

■ The trainer may create a fantasy voyage in which

the participants pilot or are passengers on an airplane. For example: a first solo flight, a pass over the Grand Canyon, a flight into a battle, etc.

_____

_____

_____

_____

_____

_____

EXTRATERRESTRIAL JOURNEY SHEET

Close your eyes and visualize a gray movie screen . . . . . . relax
. . . . . . breathe evenly, slowly, and deeply . . . . . . You are now entering
the preparation chamber and putting on your space suit. First your
boots, then your suit, and finally your helmet. Now you are slowly
walking up the ramp to enter your spacecraft. The door slides open.
Before you is an array of instruments and your padded chair. You
strap yourself into the chair. Now you count down for ignition: 6 -
5 - 4 - 3 - 2 - 1 - 0. You press the starter button. A blast of pressure
hits you from the front. You are forced back into your chair. You are
leaving Earth. Up, up, up . . . . . . against your planet's gravity
. . . . . . Now you are floating in space . . . . . . A complete quietness
surrounds you as your engines burn off. You look out and see black-
ness broken by small glimmers of light. You begin floating around
the cabin, gently rising toward the ceiling . . . . . . Remember to keep
breathing evenly, slowly, deeply . . . . . . You carefully pull yourself
back into your seat. You strap yourself in and very slowly begin your
descent. You are gradually descending more and more quickly. You
are now splashing into the ocean . . . . . . down . . . . . . down . . . . . .
and then slowly you rise to the surface. Open the hatch . . . . . . smell
the tart refreshing ocean air . . . . . . You are completely relaxed
. . . . . . When you are ready you may very slowly open your eyes.

Finger Collage

Activity Summary
This exercise asks the participants, using finger paints, to create a group mural. This activity is generally more effective when used during the later stage of the training program or session.

Training Application
Time Reference: Approximately 30 minutes.
Group Size: Best suited for a group of 20 or fewer participants.
Space Required: A large work area containing a table that is long enough to accommodate all of the participants. (Several tables may be placed end to end.)
Materials Needed: Finger paints, masking tape, old newspapers, a pad of newsprint, access to a wash basin, and a sufficient number of work shirts for all of the participants. (If possible, the participants should be asked to bring their own work shirts.)

Trainer Administration
1. The trainer begins the exercise by explaining that the participants will be using finger paints to create a large group mural.
2. The participants then gather around the long work table (or put tables end to end to form a long table). Next the group members put on their work shirts and cover the work table with old newspapers. They then tape sheets of newsprint (one for each participant) together end to end so that a long mural is formed. Pots of finger paints are then placed around the work area within easy reach of the participants.
3. The trainer explains that the group members will be painting their feelings into the mural. They are to transfer whatever creative thoughts they may have onto the paper. (The trainer can ask the participants to focus specifically on their feelings about their jobs, goals, values, etc.)
4. At a signal from the trainer, the group members put their fingers in the paint and begin the mural, each of them working until his or her section is covered with paint.
5. When the mural is finished, the participants are given a few minutes in which to walk around and view the mural's various sections. (When the mural

is completely dry, it may be hung on a wall for the remaining training sessions.)

6. The trainer may process the activity by initiating a discussion on both the stimulating and soothing effects of the act of creative expression. The activity concludes with a general cleanup of the work area.

Variations
■ The trainer may direct each participant, working individually on one sheet of newsprint instead of on one part of a mural, to express his or her feelings with the finger paints.

■ The group leader may have the participants, working individually, interpret various pieces of music, fingerpainting one sheet of newsprint for each piece. For example: "The Fountains of Rome," "Bolero," "Appalachian Spring," or a gospel, jazz, or popular piece.

Trainer's Notes
_____

_____

_____

_____

_____

_____

_____

_____

_____

Group Art

Activity Summary

This exercise asks the participants, working in small groups, to create joint works of art. This activity is generally more effective when used during the later stage of the training program or session.

Training Application

Time Reference: Approximately 15 to 20 minutes.

Group Size: Unlimited.

Space Required: An unobstructed area without tables or chairs. Several small meeting rooms or areas that provide private or semiprivate interaction are also needed.

Materials Needed: For each work group, a sheet of newsprint and several colored markers.

Trainer Administration

1. The group leader explains that the participants will work in groups to create joint works of art.
2. After dividing the participants into groups of four members each, the trainer gives each work group a sheet of newsprint and several colored markers.
3. The trainer tells the groups that after they have received their instructions, they will disperse to find rooms or areas in which each group can work in private.
4. The group leader then explains the activity. One member from each work group is to fold his or her group's paper in half and then in half again so that the paper is divided into four sections.
5. Then that person is to draw a picture in one section of the paper, while his or her fellow group members sit on the floor nearby, relax, and, with their eyes closed, think beautiful thoughts.
6. When the first person has finished a drawing, he or she is to fold the paper down so that his or her fellow group members can see only a small part of the drawing he or she has made.
7. The next group member is to continue the group's picture, drawing in another fourth of the paper, folding his or her section down, and then giving the paper to the next group member.
8. This process continues until all of the group members have done their drawings. The group

members then are to look at and comment on all four parts of their joint creation.

9. The groups may then add to their works of art by filling in the transitional areas between the four separate panels to complete the drawings.

10. When the work groups are finished, the trainer calls all of the participants together, and, one at a time, the work groups share their drawings with the entire group.

Variations   ■ The trainer may ask that each participant do a drawing on one piece of newsprint. The group members' pictures are then taped together to form one large "canvas."

■ The trainer may instruct each work group to create, instead of a drawing, a work of art from materials found in the room. For example: chairs, tables, paper, trash, each other, etc. (Private work space for each group is a necessity for this variation.)

Trainer's Notes _____

_____

_____

_____

_____

_____

_____

Ha

This exercise asks the participants to pass the word "ha" around a circle. This activity is generally more effective when used during the later stage of the training program or session.

Time Reference: Approximately 5 to 7 minutes.
Group Size: Best suited for a group of 20 or fewer participants.
Space Required: A room that has the potential for flexible seating.
Materials Needed: None.

1. The trainer first asks the group members to form a circular seating arrangement.
2. When the participants are seated, the group leader explains that the object of this game is for the participants, without laughing, to pass the word "ha" around the circle.
3. The trainer then designates one participant to be the head of the circle. That participant begins the game by saying "ha."
4. The person sitting to his or her right must repeat the "ha" and then say another "ha." The third person must say "ha, ha" and then given an additional "ha." In this manner the "ha's" continues around the circle.
5. The game ends when all of the participants, trying not to laugh (a virtual impossibility), have repeated the "ha's" that preceded them and then added their own "ha."

■ The trainer may use another word in place of "ha." For example: "yuck," "har," or "tee-hee."
■ The group leader may ask all of the participants to repeat the "ha's," stopping only to let the person whose turn it is pipe in with his or her own "ha."
■ The trainer may continue the exercise for five minutes, regardless of how many times the "ha's" go around the circle.

_____

_____

_____

**Trainer's
Notes**
continued

_____

_____

_____

_____

_____

_____

Hot Pepper

Activity Summary

This exercise challenges the participants to pass the "hot pepper" as quickly as possible. This icebreaker is effective at any time during the learning program.

Training Application

Time Reference: Approximately 5 to 10 minutes.
Group Size: Unlimited.
Space Required: A room that has the potential for flexible seating.
Materials Needed: A small object, such as a tennis ball.

Trainer Administration

1. The trainers ask the group members to form a circular seating arrangement.
2. When the participants are seated, the group leader holds up a small object, such as a tennis ball, and informs the group that this item will be used as the "hot pepper" in a game of the same name. Next the group leader asks the participants to close their eyes.
3. The group leader then gives the object to a randomly selected participant who must say the word "hot" as he or she quickly passes the object to the group member sitting to his or her right.
4. While saying the word "hot," each participant must continue to pass the object around until the trainer says the word "pepper." The person holding the object when the group leader says "pepper" must open his or her eyes and remove himself or herself from the circle. (The unfortunate group member must also remove his or her chair from the circle so that the remaining members may slightly shift their chairs to maintain a closely positioned circle.)
5. The icebreaker continues until only one participant, the winner, remains.

Variations

■ The group leader can conduct the exercise to music. When the music is playing, the participants pass the object. When the trainer stops the music, the person holding the object drops out of the game.
■ If the group contains more than 15 participants, the trainer can divide the group members into subgroups, each subgroup forming its own circle

of chairs. The winners from each subgroup then play the game together until one winner remains.

■ If the group is large, the trainer can have the participants pass two objects counterclockwise around the circle. The basic procedure in the Trainer Administration section remains the same except that on the word "pepper" two players will most likely be dropping out of the circle.

Trainer's Notes

_____

_____

_____

_____

_____

_____

_____

_____

How I Relax

Activity Summary

This exercise asks the participants to try relaxation exercises that other group members have found effective in reducing work-related stress. This activity is generally more effective when used during the later stage of the training program or session.

Training Application

Time Reference: Approximately 15 to 20 minutes.

Group Size: Unlimited.

Space Required: A room that has the potential for flexible seating and that contains adequate writing space for all of the participants. The area must be large enough to permit the unrestricted movement of the learners.

Materials Needed: For each participant, a pencil and a piece of paper.

Trainer Administration

1. After giving each participant a pencil and a piece of paper, the trainer explains that the participants will be using one another as sources from which to learn new ways to relax during times of stress.

2. The group members are instructed to think of what they do to relax themselves when they feel pressured or overwhelmed. For example: get up and walk around the office, stretch and flex their shoulder muscles, raise their arms above their heads, etc.

3. After several minutes the trainer asks the participants each to select one of the relaxers that he or she feels is extremely effective and to write down that exercise or activity in detail.

4. Next the group members are to pair off. (If necessary, one group may contain three participants.) The partners locate a semiprivate area within the room and trade exercises. The partners then try out and discuss each other's relaxers.

5. After several minutes the trainer reassembles the large group and begins a discussion in which the participants share their relaxation techniques with the entire group.

Variations

■ Following step #3 in the Trainer Administration section, the group leader may request that the participants put their pieces of paper in a box.

Each group member pulls out a relaxer which he or she then attempts to demonstrate for the entire group. Other group members may offer suggestions or assistance.

■ The trainer conducts the exercise as a group activity in which the group members brainstorm techniques that will relax them during tense situations. The entire group then participates in three or four representative relaxation activities.

Trainer's Notes

_____

_____

_____

_____

_____

_____

_____

_____

Macaroni Necklace

Activity Summary

This exercise challenges the participants to work quickly to make necklaces from uncooked macaroni. This icebreaker is effective at any time during the learning program.

Training Application

Time Reference: Approximately 10 to 15 minutes.

Group Size: Unlimited.

Space Required: An unobstructed area without tables or chairs. The room must be large enough to permit the unrestricted movement of the learners.

Materials Needed: A large amount of uncooked macaroni, a number of small bowls, and, for each participant, a four-foot length of heavy-duty string.

Trainer Administration

1. The trainer explains that the group members are going to take part in an exercise that demands speed and dexterity. They are going to make macaroni necklaces.
2. Next the group leader gives each participant a four-foot length of heavy-duty string. Each group member ties several knots at the bottom of his or her cord so that the pieces of macaroni will stay on the string.
3. The participants are then told that they will have 10 minutes in which to put as many pieces of macaroni on their strings as they can.
4. At a signal from the trainer, the exercise begins.
5. When the allotted time has elapsed, the winner is the participant who has created the longest macaroni necklace.

Variations

■ The trainer may ask the participants to find partners. The pairs must then put macaroni on an eight-foot length of string, each partner working from a different end.

■ The group leader may divide the participants into two teams. Each team's members then string as much macaroni as they can onto a 30-foot-long piece of heavy-duty string. The team that, within 10 minutes, creates the longest macaroni necklace is declared the winner.

Trainer's Notes

_____

_____

_____

_____

_____

_____

_____

_____

Marionette

Activity Summary

This exercise asks the participants to relax their bodies as they imitate the actions of string puppets. This icebreaker is effective at any time during the training program.

Training Application

Time Reference: Approximately 5 to 10 minutes .
Group Size: Unlimited.
Space Required: An unobstructed area without tables or chairs.
Materials Needed: None.

Trainer Administration

1. The trainer first tells the participants that they will be taking part in an exercise that is intended to help them loosen up and relax their bodies.
2. After asking the participants to stand and to spread out so that each of them will have a space in which to move freely, the group leader explains that the participants will be imagining that they are string puppets.
3. When the group members are in position, the trainer asks them to perform the following actions as they imagine a marionette would do them. (The trainer may need to demonstrate the first action so that the participants understand clearly the looseness with which a simple string puppet operates.)
   a. shake hands with an imaginary person
   b. do a dance step
   c. swim the breast stroke
   d. flag down an airplane
   e. change a light bulb
4. The trainer then may process the exercise through a group discussion in which the participants are encouraged to explain their feelings before, during, and after the activity.

Variations

■ The trainer may choose work-related actions for the participants to imitate as string puppets. For example: typing a letter, directing a meeting, arriving at work in the morning.
■ The group leader may ask the participant-marionettes to do simple calisthenics. For example: touch their toes, swing their arms, breath deeply, etc.

■ The trainer may instruct the participants to act as marionettes as they walk around the room and talk to one another.

Trainer's Notes

_____

_____

_____

_____

_____

_____

_____

Moody Blues

Activity Summary

This exercise asks the participants to strike poses that depict specific emotional states. This icebreaker is effective at any time during the learning program.

Training Application

Time Reference: Approximately 5 to 10 minutes.
Group Size: Unlimited.
Space Required: An unobstructed area without tables or chairs.
Materials Needed: None.

Trainer Administration

1. The trainer begins the exercise by asking the participants to stand and spread out around the room so that each group member has some space in which to move freely.
2. When the participants are in position, the group leader asks them to think about how they act or react when they are in a particular mood, i.e., the facial expressions they use, the manner in which they position their bodies, etc. Each participant is, without talking, to choose whatever mood he or she wishes.
3. The trainer then requests that each participant create, through facial expressions and body language, the mood he or she has chosen.
4. Maintaining their postures and remaining silent, the participants are to briefly mill about the room and observe the postures and moods of others.
5. Next the trainer asks each participant to depict the mood that is the opposite to the one he or she has initially shown. For example: If a participant has first depicted depression, he or she would then depict elation. Again, the group members are to maintain their postures while they walk around the room and observe others.
6. The trainer may conclude the exercise with a general discussion on how body language and facial expressions convey emotions, focusing on the specific cues the participants use to detect other people's emotional states.

Variations

■ The group leader may ask the participants, one at a time, to demonstrate their chosen emotional states in front of the entire group. The group members must then attempt to guess the participant's mood.

■ The trainer may prepare slips of paper with emotions written on them. For example: resentment, elation, shyness, jealousy, boredom, etc. The participants each receive a paper and must use facial expressions and body movements to display the emotion. The basic procedure outlined in the Trainer Administration section is followed for the exercise.

**Trainer's
Notes**

_____

_____

_____

_____

_____

_____

_____

More Motions

This exercise asks the participants, standing in a circle, to repeat movements created by other group members and then to add motions of their own. This activity is generally more effective when used during the later stage of the training program or session.

**Training
Application**

Time Reference: Approximately 15 to 20 minutes.
Group Size: Best suited for a group of 10 to 20 participants.
Space Required: An unobstructed area without tables or chairs. The room must be large enough to permit the unrestricted movement of the learners.
Materials Needed: None.

**Trainer
Administration**

1. The trainer begins by asking the participants to stand and form a large circle, allowing a space of two or three feet between group members.
2. When the large circle has been formed, the group leader explains that in this activity the participants will be repeating the actions of other participants and then adding actions of their own.
3. A volunteer is solicited to start the activity. He or she begins by creating some movement, such as waving his or her arm, touching his or her toes, etc.
4. The participant standing to his or her right must repeat the volunteer's action and then add another motion.
5. The exercise continues with each person repeating the movements of those who preceded him or her and then adding a new motion.
6. If a person forgets to repeat one of the previous movements, the game begins again with the original volunteer initiating a new action, the next person repeating the action and adding another one, and so forth.
7. If during the second round a participant who has previously forgotten some motion again forgets a movement, the other participants may help him or her remember the motions and their order.
8. The game continues until all of the participants have repeated and then added motions.

■ The trainer may instruct the group members to say any word or phrase that comes to mind as they create their particular movements. For example: A player may say "See you soon!" as he or she waves an arm, or he or she may jump up and down while saying "Where did they go!" The participants must then repeat both the actions and the words spoken by the previous group members before they can add words and motions of their own.

■ The group leader may tell the participants that the object of the game is to move up to the position of the volunteer who began the game. If a participant forgets a motion, he or she goes to the end of the circle, and the next player begins the exercise again with a new motion.

Trainer's Notes

_____

_____

_____

_____

_____

_____

_____

Musical Interpretation

This exercise asks the participants to use their bodies to interpret music. This activity is generally more effective when used during the later stage of the training program or session.

Time Reference: Approximately 15 to 20 minutes.
Group Size: Unlimited.
Space Required: An unobstructed area without tables and chairs.
Materials Needed: For the trainer, a tape player and cassette tapes or a record player and recordings of various kinds of music. (Instrumental music with a variety of rhythms is ideal.)

1. The trainer begins by telling the group members that they will be performing an exercise that is designed to help them relax their minds and bodies.

2. The group members are to stand, remove any obstacles from the room, and then spread out so that each of them has a space in which to move freely.

3. The trainer asks that the group members stand with their eyes closed while they let all conscious thoughts about problems and responsibilities float from their minds. As they begin to relax, they are to try to become acutely aware of their bodies.

4. After a minute or two, the group leader turns on the tape player and tells the participants to listen to the music. (The trainer will find that instrumental music is most appropriate for the exercise. For example: "Theme from *Star Wars,*" "Thus Spake Zarathustra," or a selection from Beethoven, Tchaikovsky, Bernstein, Mancini, etc.)

5. With their eyes still closed, the group members are to begin interpreting the music in any way they wish. They may sway their bodies, snap their fingers, tap their feet, or perform actual dances.

6. The object of the exercise is for the participants to relax and feel the beat of the music to the exclusion of all else.

7. When the piece of music ends, the trainer may play another composition or instruct the group

members to open their eyes and share with one another the feelings they have experienced. The participants may also discuss the effects music has in creating and dispelling moods.

Variations   ■ The trainer may ask the group members to pair off and work together with their partners to interpret music.
■ The group leader may instruct the participants to perform simple calisthenics to a particular piece of music.
■ The trainer may solicit a volunteer to serve as the group's leader. The volunteer directs the group members through a series of movements to music.

Trainer's Notes

_____

_____

_____

_____

_____

_____

_____

_____

Newspaper Shuffle

Activity Summary

This exercise, a quick-moving energizer, asks the participants to reorganize the pages of newspapers. This icebreaker is effective at any time during the learning program.

Training Application

Time Reference: Approximately 5 to 10 minutes.

Group Size: Unlimited.

Space Required: A room that has the potential for flexible seating.

Materials Needed: For each participant, a newspaper with its pages out of order and some pages upside down. All of the newspapers should contain the same total number of pages.

Trainer Administration

1. The trainer asks the group members to form a circular seating arrangement.
2. When the participants are seated, the group leader explains that they will be playing a game that requires them to think quickly. They will be putting the pages of newspapers in their proper order.
3. The trainer then gives each participant a mixed-up newspaper. At a signal, the group members, working in close quarters, begin to reorganize their newspapers.
4. The first person to complete the task is declared the winner.

Variations

■ The group leader may instruct the participants to put the pages of the mixed-up newspapers in reverse order.

■ The trainer may divide the group members into two teams. Representatives from each team come forward and compete against each other, the winning team in each confrontation receiving one point. When all of the team members have competed, the winner is the team with the higher score.

Trainer's Notes

_____

_____

_____

**Trainer's
Notes**
continued

_____

_____

_____

_____

_____

Potpourri of Exercises

Activity Summary

These exercises are designed to relax the participants' minds and bodies. This series of icebreakers is effective at any time during the learning program.

Training Application

Time Reference: Approximately 15 minutes for the six exercises.

Group Size: Unlimited.

Space Required: An unobstructed area without tables or chairs.

Materials Needed: None.

Trainer Administration

Calisthenics

The group members loosen up by doing two jumping jacks, five toe touchers, and five deep knee bends.

Arm Whirl

The participants stand in comfortable positions with their legs spread slightly apart. They raise their arms straight out from their bodies until their arms are parallel to the floor. After holding this position to the trainer's count of 10, the group members rotate their arms from their shoulders, making 10 large arm circles forward and 10 large circles backwards. The participants then swing their arms straight over their heads so that their arms are perpendicular to the floor; after holding this position to the count of 10, they lower their arms and dangle them below their waists.

Neck Nod

In this exercise the participants relieve tension from their necks. First they drop their heads so that their chins touch their chests. Then the group members stretch their necks to the left until their left ears almost touch their left shoulders; next they stretch their necks to the right until their right ears almost touch their right shoulders. Finally, they raise their heads as high as they can so that they feel a good deal of stretch in the fronts of their necks. The group members repeat this exercise four times.

Peek-a-boo

The participants sit on the floor in comfortable positions. The trainer then tells the group members to exercise their eyes. The participants look left, right, up, and then down, without moving their heads. Next the participants blink both eyes three times and wink three times with each eye. The group members repeat the exercise 10 times to a count established by the trainer.

Floor Roll

The participants lie on the floor and try to rid themselves of all tension by rolling their entire bodies from side to side.

Tension Release

The participants sit on the floor, remove their shoes, and begin wiggling their toes. They then place their hands on the floor for support and kick each of their legs out three or four times. Sitting in comfortable positions with their legs stretched out in front of them, the participants shake the tension out of their bodies, beginning with their legs and moving up to their trunks, their arms, and, finally, their heads.

Variation

■ Instead of using all six exercises at one time, the trainer can intersperse them, one at a time, in the training or educational event.

Trainer's Notes

_____

_____

_____

_____

_____

_____

_____

_____

Prehistoric Animals

Activity
Summary This exercise challenges the participants' creativity by asking them to construct models of prehistoric animals. This icebreaker is effective at any time during the learning program.

Training
Application *Time Reference:* Approximately 30 minutes.

Group Size: Unlimited.

Space Required: An unobstructed space containing several tables. The room must be large enough to permit the unrestricted movement of the learners.

Materials Needed: Tables, a pad of newsprint, a large bowl of dough (made from flour and water), toothpicks, pieces of cardboard cut into 12-inch squares, a selection of colored markers, tape, straws, straight pins, marshmallows, cranberries, raisins, and any other creative materials that the trainer may have available, such as pieces of sponge, colored paper, crepe paper, balloons, paper clips, etc.

Trainer
Administration 1. Prior to the exercise the group leader needs to set up a table of materials to be used during the activity.

2. The trainer informs the participants that they will be creating exhibits for the Smithsonian Institute in Washington, D.C.

3. The group leader then asks the participants to spread out around the room so that each of them has his or her own work space.

4. Next the trainer gives each participant several sheets of newsprint and one 12-inch-square piece of cardboard, which will serve as the base for the creation.

5. The trainer explains that, using any of the items from the materials table, the group members are each, within 15 minutes, to create a prehistoric creature. (The trainer should encourage the participants to let their imaginations run wild—to be as creative as possible.) They are each to secure some privacy by using the newsprint to block the other participants' view of their project. After finishing his or her model, each participant is to write on the piece of cardboard the name of the creature

and a brief explanation or why it became extinct.

6. After explaining the activity, the trainer asks the participants to begin making their prehistoric creatures.

7. When 15 minutes have elapsed, the trainer solicits a volunteer to introduce his or her exhibit. After the group members view each exhibit, they reward one another with a roaring round of applause, cheers, etc., to acknowledge the participant's creative effort. This process continues until all of the group members have shared their creations.

8. The group leader concludes the activity by giving the participants several minutes to walk around the room and view one another's creations more closely.

Variations

■ The group leader may ask the participants to find partners. Each pair is then responsible for creating, naming, and explaining a prehistoric creature.

■ If the group members are willing to take risks and appear to be quite uninhibited, the trainer may request that they pair off. Using some of the items from the materials table, one of the partners molds the other partner into an exhibit for the Smithsonian.

■ The trainer may ask that, instead of a prehistoric creature, each of the participants sculpt his or her brain and its divisions.

Trainer's Notes

_____

_____

_____

_____

_____

_____

_____

Printed Foot Race

This exercise asks the participants, working in teams, to compete in a slow-moving relay race in which they lay down, step on, and pick up sheets of newspaper. This activity is generally more effective when used during the later stage of the training program or session.

**Training
Application**

Time Reference: Approximately 10 to 20 minutes.

Group Size: Unlimited, but best suited for a group of 14 or more participants.

Space Required: A large, unobstructed area without tables or chairs.

Materials Needed: For each team, one or two newspapers (at least 10 pages in length) and one chair.

**Trainer
Administration**

1. After explaining that the group members will be taking part in a relay race, the trainer asks them to divide into two teams. (If the group is large, more teams may be formed.) Should the group contain an uneven number, one player will cover the course twice.

2. The group leader then draws an imaginary starting line and asks the teams each to line up single file behind the line.

3. Approximately 30 feet in front of the starting line the trainer places one chair for each team.

4. After giving the first person in each team's line a newspaper, the group leader explains the rules of the relay race.

   a. At a signal from the trainer, the first player in each team's line (the paper layer) puts a sheet of the newspaper on the floor, steps on it, lays down another sheet, steps on it, and so forth across the floor to just beyond the chair.

   b. When the first player has finished laying the path, the second player (the runner) carefully walks out to the chair on the path; the runner may step only on the sheets of newspaper the paper layer has put down.

   c. The runner touches the chair and then makes his or her way back to the starting line by stepping only on the newspaper.

   d. When the runner has reached the line, the

paper layer returns to the line by walking and picking up the sheets of newspaper in the reverse order to which they were laid.

e. The third and fourth players repeat directions a through d, and so forth until all of the team members have covered the course in the proscribed manner.

f. The trainer serves as the referee.

g. If a player steps on the floor instead of the newspaper, the trainer may ask the player to begin his or her part of the race again.

h. If a player picks up paper in the wrong order, the trainer may ask the player to start over.

i. The winner is the team to complete the relay first.

5. After explaining the rules, the trainer gives a signal, and the relay race begins.

6. The race continues until all of the participants have competed. The team whose members complete the race first is then declared the winner.

Variations

■ In conducting the exercise, the group leader can use sheets of 8½ x 11 paper instead of newspaper.

■ The trainer may ask the runner from each team to wear a blindfold and to follow the paper layer's verbal instructions on where to step in order to cover the course. At the chair, the two change roles, the paper layer becoming the blindfolded runner and vice versa. The runner follows the paper layer's directions to return to the starting line; picking up the newspapers the paper layer returns to the line and hands the papers to the third player. The process is repeated until all of the team members have covered the course.

Trainer's Notes

_____

_____

_____

_____

_____

_____

Statues

This exercise asks the participants to relax their minds and bodies by acting as statues. This activity is generally more effective when used during the later stage of the training program or session.

Time Reference: Approximately 10 to 15 minutes.
Group Size: Unlimited.
Space Required: An unobstructed area without tables or chairs.
Materials Needed: For the trainer, the Statues List (see the last page of this exercise).

1. The trainer asks the group members to stand and then spread out so that each of them will have a space in which to move freely.
2. Next the group leader tells the participants that they will be taking part in an exercise that is designed to help them relax their minds and bodies.
3. The trainer explains that as the name or title of a statue is called out (see Statues List), each participant is to use his or her entire body to portray or interpret what he or she feels the statue looks like and/or means. The group leader may wish to demonstrate for the group a statue entitled "Friendly Dog."
4. The trainer reads the title of the first statue, and the participants simultaneously give their interpretations. After holding their poses for five seconds, the participants are to relax their bodies as completely as possible.
5. After 10 seconds the trainer reads the next title; the participants pose and then relax. This process continues until the participants have interpreted all the statues.
6. The group leader then asks the participants to portray a statue entitled "Totally Relaxed." They hold their poses for one minute.
7. The trainer may process the activity through a brief discussion in which the participants explain how their bodies felt before and during the activity and how their bodies feel at its conclusion. The trainer may then wish to lead a discussion on work-related stress and how it affects the group members' bodies.

Variations
- The trainer may ask each group member to create his or her own statue and then give it a name. One at a time, the participants unveil their statues for the entire group.
- The group leader asks the participants to pair off and to work with their partners to create, name, and then act out statues that contain two figures. For example: "The Fight," "Tea for Two," "Tired Feet," "The Dance," etc.

Trainer's Notes

_____

_____

_____

_____

_____

_____

_____

STATUES LIST

1. "Child at Play"
2. "Anteater with Full Stomach"
3. "Runner at Starting Line"
4. "Fear"
5. "Star Gazer"

6. "Victorious Athlete"
7. "Reflection"
8. "The Dancer"
9. "Rubber Band"
10. "Cat with Cream"

Superman Relay

This exercise is an energizing relay race in which the participants put on and take off various items of clothing as they imitate Clark Kent's transformation into Superman. This icebreaker is effective at any time during the learning program.

Time Reference: Approximately 10 to 15 minutes.

Group Size: Unlimited, but best suited for a group of 20 or fewer participants.

Space Required: An unobstructed area without tables or chairs. The room must be large enough to permit the unrestricted movement of the learners.

Materials Needed: For each team, a box containing an old hat or cap, a long muffler or scarf, an old, short-sleeved man's shirt in a large size, and a large overcoat or raincoat that has seen better days.

1. The trainer first explains that the participants will be taking part in a relay race in which they imitate the transformation Clark Kent must make to become Superman.

2. Next the participants are asked to divide into two teams, with an equal number of group members of each team. (If the group contains more than 20 participants, three or more teams should be formed.) If the group contains an uneven number, a member of one of the teams will need to compete twice.

3. Each team then lines up behind a designated starting line.

4. Approximately 15 feet in front of the teams, the group leader places two boxes that each contain four items of clothing: a hat, a scarf, a shirt, and a coat.

5. The trainer then explains the rules of the game.
   a. At a signal from the trainer, the first player on each team must run to his or her team's box and over his or her own clothes put on the articles of clothing that are in the box.
   b. When the player is dressed, he or she is to run back to the line and take off the clothes.
   c. The second player then dresses in the clothes,

runs to the box, removes the clothing, places the clothes in the box, and runs back to the line to tag the next player.

d. The third player runs to the box and repeats directions a and b, the fourth player follows direction c, and so forth until all of the players have dressed and undressed themselves in the old clothes.

e. In getting dressed, a player does not have to button the shirt or the coat.

f. A player may not put on an item of clothing until the player preceding him or her has removed all of the clothing.

g. A player must be wearing all of the given garb before he or she can run back to the starting line or to the box.

6. After clarifying the rules, the trainer gives a signal, and the game begins.

7. The activity continues until all of the participants have run the Superman relay. The members of the team that finishes first are declared the "Superpersons."

Variations
■ The trainer may place more items in each team's box. For example: a necklace, a bracelet, a large pair of rubber boots, etc.

■ The group leader may position a chair for each team at the starting line and another chair next to the box 15 feet in front of the line. The chairs are then connected by a long piece of string tied to the back of one chair and extending to the back of the other one. The team members must then wear blindfolds during their turns and use the string to guide themselves in moving to and from the starting line and the box of clothes.

Trainer's Notes

The Creature

This exercise is a physical activity in which the participants, working cooperatively in small groups, use their creative capacities to form strange creatures. This activity is generally more effective when used during the later stage of the training program or session.

Time Reference: Approximately 10 to 15 minutes.
Group Size: Best suited for a group of 12 or more participants.
Space Required: An unobstructed area without tables or chairs. The room must be large enough to permit the unrestricted movement of the learners. Several small meeting rooms or areas that provide private or semiprivate interaction are also needed.
Materials Needed: None.

1. The group leader first explains that the participants will be taking part in an exercise that challenges them to use their creative resources.
2. Next the participants are to divide into work groups, with four members in each group. If necessary, one or more of the groups may contain five members.
3. The trainer explains that the members of each group will be working cooperatively to form a creature. The participants are to be as imaginative as possible in developing their creation. One of the group members will act as the creature's head, one as its body, one as its tail, and one (or two) as its arm(s) or leg(s). The creature may walk, crawl, hop, slither, etc., as long as it is able to move.
4. After explaining the directions, the trainer tells the work groups to locate an area in which they can work with some degree of privacy. They are then given five minutes in which to plan their creatures.
5. When the allotted time has elapsed, the trainer calls the work groups together and asks them, one at a time, to present their creations.
6. After all of the creatures have walked or crawled across the room, the group leader may solicit the

participants' reaction to the exercise and then focus briefly on the creative aspects of the activity.

Variations
- The trainer may ask the creatures to race one another across the room.
- The group leader may instruct the members of each work group to blindfold themselves. Wearing their blindfolds, they are to form their creature and then propel it across the room.

Trainer's Notes

_____

_____

_____

_____

_____

_____

_____

_____

Think Fast

Activity Summary

This exercise challenges the participants to think quickly to come up with nouns that begin with specific letters. This icebreaker is effective at any time during the learning program.

Training Application

Time Reference: Approximately 10 to 15 minutes.
Group Size: Best suited for a group of 10 to 20 participants.
Space Required: An unobstructed area without tables or chairs.
Materials Needed: A small object, such as a tennis ball, and a dictionary for reference.

Trainer Administration

1. The trainer asks the participants to stand and form a circle.
2. When the group members are in position, the trainer explains that they will be playing a game that requires them to think quickly.
3. A volunteer is solicited to stand in the middle of the circle and serve as the leader. The volunteer is to close his or her eyes and to keep them closed during his or her term as leader.
4. The trainer then gives a small object, such as a tennis ball, to one of the participants standing in the circle and tells the group members that when the leader says "Start," the participants are to pass the object counterclockwise (to their right) around the circle.
5. When the leader says "Stop," and calls out a letter of the alphabet, the participant holding the ball must name three nouns that begin with that letter. For example: If the leader calls out the letter "B," the participant with the object might say "Ball, boy, bush."
6. If the participant names three nouns within five seconds, the game continues with the same leader; if the participant cannot name three nouns, he or she becomes the leader.
7. The game continues for 5 to 10 minutes.

Variations

■ The trainer may serve as the leader and instruct any participant who does not name three nouns to leave the circle so that the group gradually becomes smaller and smaller. The last participant to give three nouns correctly is declared the winner.

■ The group leader may use this game as a get-acquainted exercise in which a participant must call out two other group members' names when the leader says "Stop."

■ The trainer may conduct the exercise to music. When the music begins, the participants pass the object. The trainer then stops the music and calls out a letter. The participant holding the object must give three nouns that begin with the letter. If the participant cannot do so, he or she drops out of the circle, and the trainer starts the music again.

■ The group leader may conduct the exercise as indicated in the Trainer Administration section but tell the participants that a repetition of any noun during the activity will be considered an error.

■ If the group contains more than 20 participants, the trainer may form two or more subgroups that play the game at the same time.

Trainer's Notes

_____

_____

_____

_____

_____

_____

_____

_____

Feedback and Disclosure

The icebreakers in this division focus on two very important aspects of interpersonal communication: feedback and disclosure. Feedback, the reception of corrective or evaluative information by the original source, is an essential component to understanding how others perceive us. All too often feedback is used to point out mistakes or failures rather than as a means for increasing competence and/or developing awareness. If feedback, whether positive or negative, is given and received with sensitivity and openness, it can greatly increase the value of almost any learning experience. The group leader should keep in mind that feedback is most useful when it is as specific as possible, when it is directed toward behavior(s) over which the individual has some control, when it is voluntarily sought, when it is given as soon as possible after the behavior being discussed or examined has occurred, and when the person giving the feedback assumes responsibility for it.

Disclosure, the sharing of personal thoughts and/or feelings, represents the flipside of feedback. Disclosure allows others to know us as we see ourselves. Coupled with feedback, disclosure can open the door to greater understanding and depth. Disclosure can be viewed, in terms of risk, as being on a continuum from high to low. The material in this division solicits disclosure responses that involve only mild or low risk. The degree of disclosure reached by individual members or by the group itself will vary according to the nature of the learning event, the participants' expectations, the group leader's behavior, and the icebreaker selected.

Not all learning programs will involve personal disclosure or feedback. The icebreakers in this division are flexible enough to be used as vehicles for demonstrating communication variables rather than as a means for developing ongoing interpersonal relationships between participants. An exposure, if only on a surface basis, to the concepts of feedback and disclosure can enhance the impact and relevance of the course material to be presented, regardless of the specific topic being studied.

Adjectives

**Activity
Summary** This exercise asks the participants to use adjectives to describe other participants. This icebreaker is effective at any time during the learning program.

**Training
Application** *Time Reference:* Approximately 25 to 30 minutes.

Group Size: Unlimited, but best suited for a group of 10 to 20 participants. If the group contains more than 20 participants, subgroups should be formed.

Space Required: A room that has the potential for flexible seating.

Materials Needed: For each participant, paper, a pencil, and a small box or a folder.

**Trainer
Administration** 1. The trainer asks the group members to form a circular seating arrangement.
2. When the participants are seated, the trainer gives each group member a pencil, several pieces of paper, and a small box or a folder. Then the group leader explains that the participants will be using adjectives to give feedback to one another.
3. After placing a chair in the middle of the circle, the trainer asks for a volunteer to come forward and sit in the chair. If the participants appear overly anxious, the trainer may consider serving as the first volunteer. The group leader then tells the participants to write three adjectives that they think, based upon firm knowledge or initial impressions, effectively describe the volunteer. (No talking is permitted during this time.)
4. When the participants have finished their responses, the volunteer collects the adjectives, places them in his or her box, and then returns to his or her original seat. The volunteer is not to read the adjectives until all of the participants have had an opportunity to sit in the circle.
5. After all of the group members have received their adjectives, the trainer asks the participants each to write three adjectives that they feel best describe themselves. When the participants have completed this task, the trainer instructs them to open their boxes and read their adjectives. If they wish, the participants may comment on or ask questions about their adjectives.

Variations
- The trainer can ask the group members to use the names of animals, instead of adjectives, to describe the person sitting in the middle of the circle.
- The group leader can ask the participants to form groups of three or four and to share their adjectives orally with their fellow group members.

Trainer's Notes

_____

_____

_____

_____

_____

_____

_____

_____

Alter Ego

This exercise asks the participants to serve as alter egos for each other. This activity is generally more effective when used during the later stage of the participants' training. This structured experience is most appropriate for educational programs or sessions that emphasize personal interaction among group members.

**Training
Application**

Time Reference: Approximately 15 to 20 minutes.
Group Size: Unlimited.
Space Required: A room that has the potential for flexible seating. The area must be large enough to permit the unrestricted movement of the learners.
Materials Needed: None.

**Trainer
Administration**

1. After informing the group members that they will be giving each other feedback in an unusual manner, the trainer asks the participants to divide into groups of four.

2. When the work groups have formed, the trainer explains that two of the participants in each group are to sit so that they face one another. The other two group members are to stand behind the seated participants and to serve as their "alter egos." (The trainer may need to explain the concept of "alter ego."*)

3. The group leader tells the two seated participants that they are to talk with one another about their personal or professional strengths and weaknesses.

4. After three minutes the two "alter egos" repeat the conversation, each one interpreting what the person sitting in front of him or her *really* wanted to say but did not.

5. When the "alter egos" have finished their revealing conversations, the trainer asks that the four group members change places; the participants who were seated now become the "alter egos," and the exercise is repeated.

6. After the exercise has been completed, the members of each work group are to discuss the activity and their feelings about the accuracy of the statements made by their "alter egos."

Variations

■ Instead of following step #3 in the Trainer Administration section, the trainer may instruct the group members who are seated each to discuss what he or she perceives to be the other person's personal or professional strengths and weaknesses.

■ The group leader may conduct the exercise in front of the entire group, using four participants at a time.

Trainer's Notes

_____

_____

_____

_____

_____

_____

_____

_____

*Alter ego refers to a second self. In this case, the person assuming his or her partner's alter ego attempts to go beyond the surface meaning of the words used in the interaction in order to focus on the basic feelings and thoughts behind what is being exchanged. Oftentimes the alter ego will focus on issues that are intentionally omitted from the exchange or that are guarded by the individual.

Autobiographical Sheets

This exercise asks the participants, working in small groups, to use lines clipped from newspapers to help their fellow group members prepare brief autobiographies. This directed experience is best implemented after the participants have had some opportunity to engage in feedback and disclosure during the learning program.

Time Reference: Approximately 25 to 30 minutes.
Group Size: Unlimited, but best suited for a group of 12 or more participants.
Space Required: A room that has the potential for flexible seating. The area must be large enough to permit the unrestricted movement of the learners.
Materials Needed: Old newspapers, rolls of tape, and, for each participant, a sheet of newsprint and a pair of scissors.

1. The trainer first explains that the group members will be helping each other compose brief autobiographies.
2. Next the participants are asked to divide into groups of four to six members each. (If the group contains less than 12 participants, smaller work groups may be formed.) Each work group then locates a work space within the room.
3. The group leader gives each work group a stack of newspapers and a roll of tape. Each participant then receives a sheet of newsprint and a pair of scissors.
4. Next each group member writes his or her name at the top of the sheet of newsprint. All of the papers are then spread out on a table or taped to a wall so that there is immediate, unrestricted access to each sheet.
5. From the newspapers the participants clip key words, phrases, or sentences that, based upon their perceptions or impressions, describe other members of their work group. Each participant must select at least five descriptive words, phrases, or sentences for each group member's sheet. (More than three key words, phrases, or sentences may be chosen for each participant.)

6. When all of the group members have received their lines and taped them to their papers, the work groups study and then discuss their autobiographical sheets.
7. The trainer may conclude the exercise with a full-group discussion in which the participants comment on the differences between self-perceptions and the impressions received by others.

Variations
■ The trainer may ask the group members, working individually, to write brief autobiographies.

■ The group leader may ask the participants to form pairs. Each partner then clips lines that, based on his or her perceptions or impressions, describe his or her partner.

■ The trainer can direct the work group members to select lines that answer questions dealing with work-related issues. For example: "How do you view other group members as supervisors?" or "How do you evaluate the management style of your fellow group members?"

Trainer's Notes

_____

_____

_____

_____

_____

_____

_____

_____

Baggy Faces

Activity Summary

This exercise asks the participants to draw self-portraits. This icebreaker is effective at any time during the learning program.

Training Application

Time Reference: Approximately 15 to 20 minutes.
Group Size: Unlimited.
Space Required: An unobstructed area without tables or chairs.
Materials Needed: For each participant, a paper bag and at least three colored markers.

Trainer Administration

1. After informing the participants that they are going to take part in an activity that is designed to test their perceptions of themselves, the trainer gives each group member a paper bag and three or more colored markers.
2. The group leader asks the participants to place the bags over their heads and then quickly but carefully to mark and tear eyeholes for themselves. The trainer explains that, with the bags still on their heads, the participants are to draw their faces as they imagine them to be; they are to pay attention to such details as hair style, nose shape, mouth size, eye color, etc.
3. As they perform this task, the group members are not to look in mirrors or to remove the bags from their heads (unless they feel too claustrophobic).
4. When the participants have finished their self-portraits, the trainer asks them to mingle with their fellow group members and to discuss the importance of self-perception.
5. After several minutes, the group leader tells the participants to remove and examine their masks. The trainer can solicit reactions to the experience and then begin a general discussion on the impact of self-perceptions on the participants' personal and professional lives.

Variations

■ The trainer may ask the participants to form pairs. On his or her bag, each partner would then draw his or her partner's face. The partners would then discuss the accuracy of their perceptions of each other.

■ The group leader may instruct the participants to draw their own faces before they place the bags on their heads. Then they complete steps #4 and 5 in the Trainer Administration section.

■ The trainer may give each participant tape, string, and a variety of odds and ends. The group members are then to be as imaginative as possible in decorating their bags to "capture" their fantasy selves. For example: String can be used as hair, straws for ears, buttons for dimples, etc. The masks are to be created in private and then worn for display.

Trainer's Notes

_____

_____

_____

_____

_____

_____

_____

Behind Your Back

Activity Summary

This exercise asks the participants to pair off and to share information about themselves with their partners. Since this directed experience is best implemented after the participants have had some opportunity to engage in feedback and disclosure, the activity is generally more effective when used during the later stage of the participants' training. This structured experience is most appropriate for educational programs or sessions that emphasize personal interaction among the group members.

Training Application

Time Reference: Approximately 15 to 20 minutes.

Group Size: Unlimited.

Space Required: A room that has the potential for flexible seating. The area must be large enough to permit the unrestricted movement of the learners.

Materials Needed: None.

Trainer Administration

1. After briefly explaining the concept of feedback,* the trainer informs the participants that during this exercise they will be sharing information about themselves.
2. Next the group leader asks that the participants form pairs and then spread out around the room so that each pair has some degree of privacy.
3. The partners are instructed to sit on the floor facing each other and to give feedback on how they perceive each other. (General impressions can be used.) Neither of the partners may ask questions about or respond to the other person's statements. (The trainer may ask the participants to focus of feedback regarding a specific skill or characteristic that is pertinent to the topic under study.)
4. After five minutes the group leader tells the partners to sit back to back. The partners then respond to the feedback they have received from each other and ask any questions they wish.
5. When another five minutes have elapsed, the trainer asks the partners to return to the group, where they then share their reactions to and thoughts about the exercise.

Variations   ■ The trainer may request that the partners begin the exercise sitting back to back. Asking no questions of each other and responding to no statements about themselves, the partners give feedback on how they perceive each other. After five minutes the partners face each other and discuss the accuracy of their perceptions.

■ The group leader asks the partners to sit facing each other and to make various statements about how they perceive themselves. Sitting back to back, the partners then comment on or ask questions about each other's self-perceptions.

Trainer's Notes

_____

_____

_____

_____

_____

_____

_____

_____

*The trainer may wish to remind the group members that feedback is most effectiv when (1) it is specific, (2) it is directed toward behavior over which the person has som control, (3) it is voluntarily sought, (4) it is given as soon as possible after the behavic has occurred, and (5) the person giving the feedback assumes responsibility for it.

Body Expression

This exercise explores nonverbal behavior by asking the participants to use specific parts of their bodies to express certain emotions. This structured experience is most appropriate for educational programs or sessions that emphasize personal interaction among group members.

Time Reference: Approximately 15 to 20 minutes.

Group Size: Unlimited. If the group contains more than 20 participants, subgroups should be formed.

Space Required: An unobstructed area without tables and chairs.

Materials Needed: For each participant, a trainer-prepared slip of paper naming an emotion and a body part (see Emotions and Body Parts List on the last page of this exercise).

1. The group leader begins the exercise by asking the participants to stand and form a circle.
2. When the group members are in position, the trainer explains that they will be using various parts of their bodies to portray different emotions.
3. The group leader then gives each participant a slip of paper upon which is written an emotion and the name of a part of the body (see Emotions and Body Parts List). At this time the group members are not to share their emotions and body parts with their fellow participants.
4. The group leader solicits a volunteer to begin the activity. The volunteer acts out his or her emotion, and the other group members have 30 seconds in which to identify the emotion being portrayed. Repeating this procedure, the participants, one at a time, use their designated body part to express their assigned emotion.
5. When all of the participants have portrayed their assigned emotions, the trainer initiates a brief discussion on the nonverbal expression of emotion and its relationship to the participants' professional and/or personal environments.

Variations   ■ The group leader can encourage each participant to use gutteral sounds that correspond to the emotion he or she is portraying.
■ The trainer can ask the group members to mill around the room as they simultaneously display their assigned emotions.

Trainer's Notes

_____

_____

_____

_____

_____

_____

_____

_____

EMOTIONS AND BODY PARTS LIST

1. Love — Feet
2. Frustration — Eyes
3. Anger — Hands
4. Fear — Mouth
5. Disgust — Arms
6. Surprise — Hands
7. Sadness — Mouth
8. Hate — Fingers
9. Reverence — Arms
10. Sorrow — Shoulders

11. Impatience — Feet
12. Boredom — Legs
13. Exasperation — Eyes
14. Tenderness — Hands
15. Excitement — Mouth
16. Loathing — Arms
17. Exhaustion — Waist
18. Joyfulness — Fingers
19. Terror — Mouth
20. Puzzlement — Shoulders

Dimensions of Trust

Activity Summary This exercise asks the participants to brainstorm actions that create trust. Generally more effective when used in the early stage of the group's formation, this structured experience is most appropriate for educational programs or sessions that emphasize personal interaction among group members.

Training Application

Time Reference: Approximately 15 to 20 minutes.

Group Size: Unlimited.

Space Required: A room that is large enough to accommodate the comfortable seating of the participants.

Materials Needed: A blackboard or a pad of newsprint, a piece of chalk or a black marker, and masking tape.

Trainer Administration

1. The group leader begins by requesting that the participants think about what the word "trust" means to them.
2. After several minutes the trainer asks the group members to brainstorm actions or personal characteristics that they feel build or promote trust. For example: maintaining confidentialities, being dependable, having a caring manner, being understanding, etc.
3. The trainer lists these actions and characteristics on a blackboard or newsprint.
4. Then the group members are to brainstorm *specific* actions and characteristics that can help them build trust in one another during this particular training session or program.
5. The trainer lists these on the blackboard or newsprint and asks the group members to incorporate some of the actions or behaviors into the remainder of the training session or program.
6. The group leader may conclude the exercise with a brief discussion of trust in the personal or professional setting.

Variations

■ The trainer may direct the participants, working individually, to rate themselves on a scale of 1 to 10 on the actions and characteristics they have listed as being important in building and maintaining trust (1 indicating poor and 10 indicating excellent).

■ The group leader may ask the participants to form pairs and, with their partners, to brainstorm actions and characteristics that promote or build trust. Then the trainer reassembles the group, and the pairs share their thoughts with their fellow participants.

■ The trainer may request that the participants form work groups of five or six individuals each. Each work group formulates its definition of the word "trust," and its members then identify those factors that inhibit or promote the development of trust in the personal or professional setting. Next each work group reports on its discussion for the entire group.

**Trainer's
Notes**

_____

_____

_____

_____

_____

_____

_____

_____

Impressions

This exercise asks the participants to share their initial impressions of one another. Most effective when used in the early stage of the group's formation, this directed experience is generally more appropriate for educational programs or sessions that emphasize personal interaction among the group members.

Time Reference: Approximately 30 to 40 minutes.

Group Size: Unlimited, but best suited for a group of 15 or fewer participants. (If the group contains more than 15 participants, more time will be required to complete the exercise.)

Space Required: A room that has the potential for flexible seating.

Materials Needed: For each participant, a pencil and a copy of the Impressions Sheet (see the last page of this exercise).

1. The group leader begins by asking the participants to form a circular seating arrangement.
2. When the group members are seated, the trainer tells them that in this activity they will receive feedback on the way they are initially perceived by others.
3. Next the trainer explains that each participant will be introducing himself or herself to the group. During the introduction, the individual is to give his or her name and then spend approximately one minute telling anything he or she would like about his or her life. Following each introduction, the other group members will be given an opportunity to ask brief questions about or to request clarification on anything the individual has said.
4. After explaining the exercise, the group leader asks for a volunteer to begin the introductions. When the volunteer has completed his or her introduction and has answered any questions the group members have posed, the participant to his or her right gives the next introduction, and so on around the circle.
5. When all of the participants have introduced themselves, the trainer gives each group member a pencil and a copy of the Impressions Sheet. The

group leader then asks the participants to fill out the form by writing in each group member's name and noting their initial impressions of that person. (To refresh the participants' memories, the leader may ask each group member to repeat his or her name one more time.) The trainer should inform the group members that they will be reading their written reactions to the group.

6. When all of the participants have completed the forms, the group leader asks for a volunteer to receive feedback from the other participants on their initial impressions of him or her. Each group member then reads out loud his or her impressions of the volunteer. When the volunteer has received all of the feedback, he or she may comment briefly on, or give his or her reactions to, what has been said. A new volunteer is then sought, and the process is repeated.

7. The activity continues until all of the participants have received feedback on the other group members' initial impressions of them.

Variations
■ After the exercise has been completed, the trainer may request that the participants mill about the room and discuss their reactions to the feedback they have received.

■ The group leader may conclude the exercise with a discussion on perceptions and their relationship to how individuals project themselves in their initial impressions of others.

Trainer's Notes

IMPRESSIONS SHEET

GROUP MEMBERS' NAMES   IMPRESSIONS

1. _____ _____

      _____

2. _____ _____

      _____

3. _____ _____

      _____

4. _____ _____

      _____

5. _____ _____

      _____

6. _____ _____

      _____

7. _____ _____

      _____

8. _____ _____

      _____

9. _____ _____

      _____

0. _____ _____

      _____

IMPRESSIONS SHEET (continued)

GROUP MEMBERS' NAMES   IMPRESSIONS

11. _____   _____

_____

12. _____   _____

_____

13. _____   _____

_____

14. _____   _____

_____

15. _____   _____

_____

In the Oval Office

Activity Summary

This exercise asks the participants to list their qualifications for becoming President of the United States. Since this self-affirming experience is best implemented after the participants have had some opportunity to engage in feedback and disclosure, the activity is generally more effective when used during the later stage of the training program or session.

Training Application

Time Reference: Approximately 15 to 20 minutes.

Group Size: Unlimited, but best suited for a group of 10 to 20 participants. If the group contains more than 20 participants, subgroups should be formed.

Space Required: A room that contains adequte writing space for all of the participants.

Materials Needed: For each participant, a pencil and a piece of paper.

Trainer Administration

1. After giving each participant a pencil and a piece of paper, the trainer explains that in this exercise the group members are all candidates for President of the United States.
2. The group leader then asks the participants to list their qualifications for office, basing their comments upon their self-perceptions, so that their campaign managers can begin to prepare their campaigns.
3. After five minutes, the trainer asks for a volunteer, who, assuming the role of his or her own campaign manager, then reads his or her list of qualifications to the entire group.
4. The activity continues until all of the participants have read their lists.
5. The group members may then vote to determine the person who, based on the lists and the manner in which they were presented, they feel would make a good President.
6. The trainer may then lead a general discussion on self-perception and its relationship to one's personal and/or professional impact.

Variations

■ The trainer may ask the participants to pair off, one partner becoming the candidate and the other partner assuming the role of campaign manager. The campaign managers interview their candidates, list their qualifications, and present campaign speeches to the group. The partners then reverse roles and repeat the exercise.

■ The group leader may request that instead of reading their lists of qualifications, the participants individually formulate and then present campaign speeches that outline their qualifications for office.

Trainer's Notes

_____

_____

_____

_____

_____

_____

_____

_____

Know Your Neighbor

Activity Summary

This exercise gives the participants an opportunity to learn how their fellow group members perceive others and themselves. This directed experience is best implemented after the participants have had some opportunity to engage in feedback and disclosure during the learning program.

Training Application

Time Reference: Approximately 25 to 30 minutes.

Group Size: Best suited for a goup of 20 or fewer participants. If the group contains more than 20 participants, subgroups should be formed.

Space Required: A room that has the potential for flexible seating.

Materials Needed: None.

Trainer Administration

1. The trainer asks the group members to form a circular seating arrangement.
2. When the participants are seated, the group leader explains that they will be engaging in an activity that will help them learn more about one another.
3. The trainer then solicits a volunteer to assume the role of leader. The volunteer is to select one group member and ask him or her a personal question. For example: "Do you like to spend most of your time with others?" or "Do you enjoy attention?"
4. The participant to whom the question is addressed is not to respond; instead, the person sitting to his or her right answers the question, basing the answer on his or her perceptions of the person to whom the question was directed.
5. The leader continues around the circle, asking questions of and receiving answers about all of the participants.
6. The trainer then selects a new leader. The exercise continues, this time with the person to the left answering for the participant to whom a question is addressed.
7. This procedure is repeated until all of the group members have had an opportunity to assume the role of leader.
8. When the exercise has been completed, the group members discuss their thoughts and feelings about how others perceive them.

Variations ■ The participant to whom a question has been addressed may interrupt the neighbor if he or she feels that the question is being answered incorrectly.

■ The neighbors to the right and left of the person being asked a question may both respond, or all of the group members may answer the question.

Trainer's Notes _____

_____

_____

_____

_____

_____

_____

_____

Life Map

Activity Summary

This exercise asks the participants to prepare a map that records and explains the significant events in their lives. This activity is generally more effective when used in the early stage of the group's formation.

Training Application

Time Reference: Approximately 25 to 30 minutes.

Group Size: Unlimited.

Space Required: A room that is large enough to permit the unrestricted movement of the participants.

Materials Needed: For each participant, at least two sheets of newsprint, two or three colored markers; for the trainer, a copy of the Sample Life Map (see the last page of this exercise).

Trainer Administration

1. The trainer asks the group members to reflect upon the significant events in their lives, beginning with the important events of their childhoods and continuing up to the present time.

2. While the group members are thinking about their pasts, the trainer gives each participant several sheets of newsprint and two or three colored markers. The group leader then requests that on one sheet of newsprint the participants each list their significant events in the order in which they occurred. (The participants should spread out around the room so that they each may have some degree of privacy.)

3. The trainer then asks that the group members use their notes to prepare maps that reflect the events that have led them to their present point in life. The group leader further explains that in preparing their maps the participants are to be as creative as possible (see Sample Life Map as one possible option). The trainer tells the participants that they have approximately 10 minutes to complete their maps.

4. When the allotted time has elapsed, the group leader asks the participants to pair off and then discuss their maps with their partners.

Variations
■ The trainer may ask the group members to prepare maps of their careers or of the significant events in the past year.

■ When the participants have completed the steps in the Trainer Administration section, the trainer may ask them to put their names on their maps and then tape them up around the room so that they can be shared with and discussed by everyone in the group.

Trainer's Notes

_____

_____

_____

_____

_____

_____

_____

_____

SAMPLE LIFE MAP

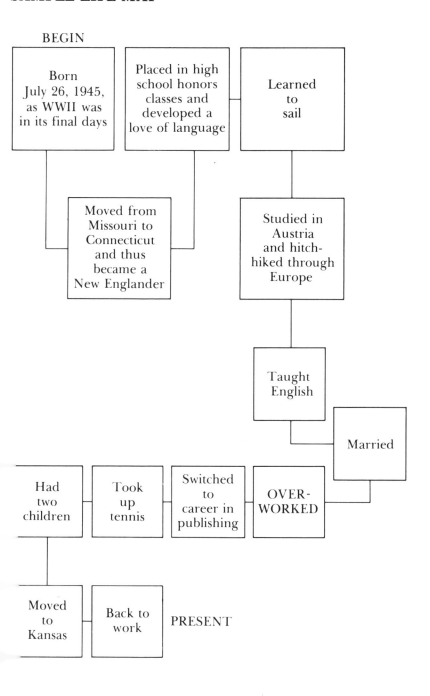

BEGIN

Born July 26, 1945, as WWII was in its final days	Placed in high school honors classes and developed a love of language	Learned to sail

Moved from Missouri to Connecticut and thus became a New Englander

Studied in Austria and hitch-hiked through Europe

Taught English

Married

Had two children	Took up tennis	Switched to career in publishing	OVER-WORKED

Moved to Kansas	Back to work	PRESENT

Like/Dislike

Activity Summary This exercise is designed to test the participants' self-perceptions as they examine what they most like and most dislike about themselves. Since this directed experience is best implemented after the participants have had some opportunity to engage in feedback and disclosure, the activity is generally more effective when used during the later stage of the training program or session.

Training Application

Time Reference: Approximately 25 to 30 minutes.

Group Size: Best suited for a group of 10 to 20 participants. If the group contains more than 20 participants, subgroups should be formed.

Space Required: A room that contains adequate writing space for all of the participants. The area must be large enough to permit the unrestricted movement of the learners.

Materials Needed: For each participant, a pencil and a piece of paper.

Trainer Administration

1. The trainer begins the exercise by explaining that the participants will be examining the ways in which they perceive themselves and are, in turn, perceived by others.

2. After distributing pencils and paper to all of the group members, the trainer asks the participants to write down three characteristics, traits, talents, etc. that they like most about themselves and three characteristics, behaviors, traits, etc. that they most dislike in themselves.

3. When they have completed this task, the participants are instructed, one at a time, to read their lists to the entire group. After each participant has shared his or her list, the other group members briefly discuss their perceptions of that group member.

4. After all of the participants have shared their lists, the group leader may lead a general discussion on perceptions of self and others.

Variations

■ The trainer may ask the participants to write down what they like and dislike in people in general or what they most like and dislike to do for enjoyment or pleasure.

■ The group leader may request that the participants hand in their lists without signing them. The group members then each select a list at random and, after reading it out loud to the group, attempt to guess whose list it is. The participants may be asked to explain the reasons for their guesses.

Trainer's Notes

_____

_____

_____

_____

_____

_____

_____

_____

Off Your Chest

Activity Summary This exercise gives the participants an opportunity to fantasize a one-sided conversation with someone with whom they have been or are presently in conflict. This directed experience is best implemented after the participants have had some opportunity to engage in feedback and disclosure during the learning program.

Training Application

Time Reference: Approximately 5 to 10 minutes.
Group Size: Unlimited.
Space Required: A room that has the potential for flexible seating.
Materials Needed: None.

Trainer Administration

1. The group leader explains that, working individually, the participants are going to have an opportunity to relieve themselves of some personal pressure.
2. Each participant is to move his or her chair to a place in the room where he or she can be somewhat apart from other group members.
3. When the group members are seated, the trainer asks each of them to close his or her eyes and to envision a person with whom he or she is having or has had a serious conflict.
4. Each group member is then silently to imagine a one-sided conversation in which he or she tells that person his or her real feelings. In the conversation the group member can concentrate on how he or she feels about the person or the person's actions and can tell the person anything he or she has wished but for some reason has been unable to say. The person in each participant's fantasy is not to respond to what the participant says.
5. After two minutes the trainer asks the group members to conclude their imaginary conversations and to begin thinking pleasant thoughts. For example: pleasant thoughts about a cool, wooded glen, the rhythm of ocean waves breaking on a beach, the beauty of the sky and earth as viewed from the top of a high hill, etc.

6. The trainer may process the activity through a sharing of experiences and a discussion of the cleansing benefits of this type of activity.

Variations
■ The trainer may ask each group member to include in his or her fantasy the responses of the person with whom he or she is in conflict; thus, the fantasy becomes a two-way conversation.

■ The group leader may ask that in his or her fantasy each participant use body language and facial expressions to express his or her grievances to the person involved in the conflict.

■ The trainer may give the group members the option of actually talking during the activity. The room, however, must be large enough to ensure some degree of privacy for each participant.

Trainer's Notes

_____

_____

_____

_____

_____

_____

_____

_____

On the Ledge

This exercise explores the issue of trust as the participants, using a hypothetical situation in which they must spend the night on a cliff ledge, are asked to trust one another "with their lives." This structured experience is most appropriate for educational programs or sessions that emphasize personal interaction among group members. This icebreaker is effective at any time during the learning program.

Time Reference: Approximately 10 to 15 minutes.

Group Size: Best suited for a group of 12 or more participants.

Space Required: An unobstructed area without tables or chairs. The room must be large enough to permit the unrestricted movement of the learners.

Materials Needed: For each work group, a piece of chalk or a 16-foot length of string.

1. The group leader begins the exercise by explaining that the participants will be engaged in an activity that depends upon the trust they place in one another.
2. The participants are then to break into work groups of four or five members each. Each work group is to locate its own space within the room.
3. Next the trainer gives each group a piece of chalk or a 16-foot length of string and asks that each group mark off or construct a space that is approximately five feet long and three feet wide.
4. When all of the groups have completed this task, the trainer explains that the space each subgroup has marked is the size of a cliff's ledge, 300 feet above the ground, upon which the members of the subgroup are stranded. They will be rescued in the morning, but they must first make it through the night on the ledge. The members of each group must find a way for all of them to sleep so that no one falls off the ledge during the night. If any group member's body extends over the line, he or she is doomed.
5. The subgroups are then given several moments in which to arrange themselves in sleeping positions that they can hold for three minutes.

6. When the allotted three minutes have elapsed, the trainer calls the groups together and asks them to discuss this exercise briefly. The participants then share the feelings they think they would have if they were really forced to spend the night together on the edge of a cliff.
7. The trainer concludes the activity with a general discussion on trust, i.e., how it is formed, its impact on one's personal and professional environment, the values and assumptions associated with trust, etc.

Variations
■ The trainer may ask that each workgroup choose a leader to be responsible for the group members' sleeping arrangements and overall safety.
■ The group leader may request that the participants pair off and perform the exercise together on a "cliff edge" that is two feet wide and three feet long.
■ The trainer may, at his or her discretion, join one or several of the subgroups and thus increase the odds that some group member will "fall."

Trainer's Notes
_____
_____
_____
_____
_____
_____
_____
_____

Role Throwaway

This exercise asks the participants to examine the various roles they assume in their lives and then to determine the importance of each role. This structured experience is most appropriate for educational programs or sessions that emphasize personal interaction among group members. This icebreaker is effective at any time during the learning program.

Time Reference: Approximately 25 to 30 minutes.

Group Size: Unlimited, but best suited for a group of 12 or fewer participants. If the group contains more than 12 participants, subgroups should be formed.

Space Required: A room that has the potential for flexible seating.

Materials Needed: For each participant, a pencil and a piece of paper.

1. The group leader begins the exercise by asking the participants to form a circular seating arrangement.
2. When the participants are seated, the trainer gives each group member a pencil and a piece of paper. The group leader then explains that the participants will be examining the roles they have assumed and the importance they attach to each role.
3. The group leader tells the participants to fold their pieces of paper in half and then in half again so that the paper is divided into four sections. After unfolding their papers, the group members are to write, one to a section, four roles that they assume in their lives. For example: supervisor, husband, father, coach; or breadwinner, daughter, artist, lover.
4. When the participants have completed this task, each of them is to examine his or her four roles carefully and to briefly share and discuss the roles with other group members.
5. Then each group member, pretending to rid his or her life of a role, tears off one section of his or her paper and throws it into the middle of the circle.

6. When the participants have all thrown away a section of their paper, the trainer asks them how they would feel if they could really throw away a role. What impact would doing so have upon their lives?
7. The participants repeat steps #5 and 6 until they have discarded all four roles.
8. The trainer may process the activity through a group discussion of the impact of the roles they assume, i.e., difficulties, responsibilities, demands, etc.

Variations

■ If the group contains more than 12 persons, the group leader may divide the group into small work groups of four or five persons. The participants then work in groups to complete steps #5, 6, and 7 in the Trainer Administration section. The trainer then reassembles the large group and initiates a discussion of the exercise.

■ The group leader may request that all four roles relate to the participants' occupations. For example: subordinate, supervisor, co-worker, salesperson.

■ The trainer may have the participants perform steps #1 through 4 in the Trainer Administration section. Then the group members throw all four roles into the center of the circle. Next the participants scramble through the pile until they find four roles they would like to keep. They may, of course, select roles that their fellow members have listed. The trainer then initiates a discussion in which the participants share their feelings about the exercise.

Trainer's Notes

_____

_____

_____

_____

_____

_____

_____

_____

Royal Family

This exercise asks the participants to draw coats of arms that describe themselves and their lives. This structured experience is most appropriate for educational programs or sessions that emphasize personal interaction among group members. This icebreaker is effective at any time during the learning program.

Time Reference: Approximately 15 to 20 minutes.
Group Size: Unlimited.
Space Required: A room that contains adequate writing space for all of the participants. The area must be large enough to permit the unrestricted movement of the learners.
Materials Needed: For each participant, a piece of paper, three or four colored pencils or markers, and a piece of masking tape; for the trainer, a copy of the Sample Coat of Arms (see the last page of this exercise).

1. The group leader explains that the participants will each be drawing a coat of arms that represents or depicts his or her life.
2. While the trainer gives each participant a piece of paper and three or four colored pencils or markers, the group members are to think of various symbols, animals, and/or sayings that describe themselves and their lives.
3. The group leader then displays the Sample Coat of Arms and explains the possible meaning of each of its parts. The participants are then given 10 minutes in which to prepare their own coats of arms.
4. When the allotted time has elapsed, the group leader asks the participants to mill about the room, displaying their coats of arms and providing explanations of the symbols and sayings they have used.

■ If the group contains 15 or fewer members, the trainer may ask each participant to share and discuss his or her coat of arms with the entire group.

- The group leader may instruct the participants to form pairs and then discuss their coats of arms with their partners.
- The trainer may request that the participants tape their drawings up around the room. The group members would then review the various coats of arms and attempt to guess to whom each one belongs.

Trainer's Notes

SAMPLE COAT OF ARMS

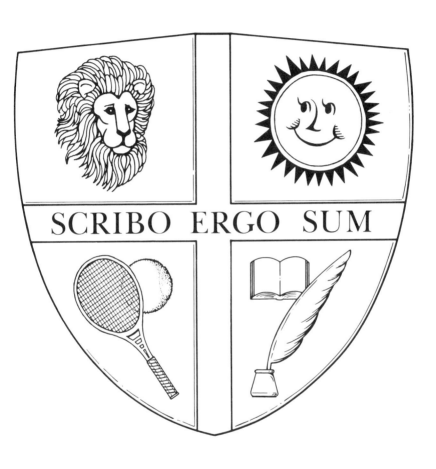

SCRIBO ERGO SUM

Sculptor

This exercise asks that the participants, using their fellow group members as "clay," create sculptures that represent events in their lives. This directed experience is best implemented after the participants have had some opportunity to engage in feedback and disclosure during the learning program.

Time Reference: Approximately 25 to 30 minutes.
Group Size: Best suited for a group of 10 to 20 participants.
Space Required: An unobstructed area without tables or chairs. The room must be large enough to permit the unrestricted movement of the learners.
Materials Needed: None.

1. The trainer instructs the group members to form a circular seating arrangement.
2. When the participants are seated, the trainer asks them to think of one key event or moment in their lives, a happening that has had some significant impact on the persons they have become and/or the professional positions they currently hold.
3. The trainer then explains that each participant is to create a sculpture that depicts or represents his or her important event. As sculptor, the participant is to use his or her fellow group members as "clay," and to position as many of them as necessary into a sculpture that captures his or her key moment. The trainer further explains that when each participant has finished his or her creation, he or she is to tell the group about the event and how it relates to the sculpture.
4. The trainer then solicits a volunteer to come to the center of the circle and begin the exercise. (If the group members appear overly anxious or inhibited, the trainer may consider being the first volunteer.) The volunteer selects as many group members as are necessary to sculpt the event or moment. Without speaking, the volunteer begins to physically move the chosen group members into the desired positions. When the volunteer has completed and then discussed the sculpture, the individuals in the sculpture return to their seats

with the volunteer. A new volunteer comes forward to sculpt his or her key event.

5. The activity continues until all of the participants have presented and discussed their sculptures.

Variations

■ The trainer may specify that the event to be sculpted be chosen from one specific area or time period in the participants' lives: their professional situations, their educational experiences, their childhoods, etc.

■ The trainer may adapt the activity to a larger group by breaking the participants into work groups of five members each.

■ The trainer may ask that each participant use only himself or herself in creating the sculpture.

Trainer's Notes

_____

_____

_____

_____

_____

_____

_____

_____

' Stranded

This exercise asks the participants each to choose five well-known individuals who possess valued qualities or characteristics that make them desired companions on a desert island. This icebreaker is effective at any time during the learning program.

Time Reference: Approximately 15 to 20 minutes.

Group Size: Unlimited, but best suited for a group of 10 to 20 participants.

Space Required: A room that is large enough to accommodate the comfortable seating of the participants.

Materials Needed: For each participant, a pencil and a piece of paper.

1. The group leader first explains that in this activity the participants will be asked to identify the valued characteristics or qualities found in others.

2. While giving each group member a pencil and a piece of paper, the trainer asks that each of them imagine that he or she is stranded alone on a desert island.

3. Keeping in mind that there is much to be done to create a hospitable environment on the island, each group member is then to write on a piece of paper the names of five well-known persons, i.e., politicians, movie stars, inventors, artists, etc., with whom he or she would like to be stranded. If he or she wishes, a participant may bring historical or fictional figures to life by writing their names on the list.

4. When the group members have completed their lists, the trainer asks that next to each of the five names, the participant note the characteristics or qualities the individual possesses that make him or her a dependable companion on the desert island.

5. After five minutes the group leader solicits volunteers to share with the entire group the specific characteristics their famous individuals possess.

6. The trainer may process the activity through a discussion in which the participants point out the

similarities and differences among the various volunteers' lists of valued characteristics or qualities. In addition, the group members should be queried on whether or not those people most closely involved with them in their personal and/or professional lives possess those characteristics or qualities they have identified.

Variations
■ The trainer may direct the participants to choose five well-known individuals to help them rebuild a society.

■ After the completion of step #3 in the Trainer Administration section, the group leader may ask the participants to write down the names of five individuals with whom they would *not* wish to be stranded and to explain the rationales for their choices.

Trainer's Notes

_____

_____

_____

_____

_____

_____

_____

_____

The Look

This exercise asks the participants to use facial expressions and body movements to represent or imitate specific "looks." This icebreaker is effective at any time during the learning program.

Time Reference: Approximately 5 to 10 minutes.
Group Size: Unlimited.
Space Required: An unobstructed area without tables or chairs. The room must be large enough to permit the unrestricted movement of the learners.

Materials Needed: For the trainer, the preprepared Sample Postures List (see the last page of this exercise).

1. The group leader begins the exercise by explaining that the participants will be using facial expressions and body movements to emulate specific attitudes/feelings/emotions. The trainer may wish to model a "look," such as the "I Don't Care Look," for the group members.
2. The participants are instructed to stand and begin milling about the room. The trainer explains that when he or she calls out a specific "look" (see Sample Postures List), the participants are to continue walking but are to use facial expressions and body movements that capture or represent the given "look."
3. The trainer reads the first item on the Sample Postures List, allowing the participants 20 seconds in which to emulate the "look" as they mill about the room. The trainer then reads the second item and gives the group members 20 seconds to capture the "look," and so forth for the rest of the "looks" on the list.
4. When all of the "looks" have been interpreted, the trainer concludes the exercise with a discussion in which the participants tell how each posture felt to them and, more generally, how other people's looks affect them in their professional setting(s).

■ The trainer may ask the group members to brainstorm other possible "looks" and then, working in pairs or small groups, to present the "looks" to the entire group.

■ If the participants know each other well, the group leader may request that they suggest and then act out "looks" that are typical of specific group members.

■ The trainer may also ask that as the participants walk around the room, they give "looks" that represent their attitudes toward their present work setting(s).

Trainer's Notes

_____

_____

_____

_____

_____

_____

_____

SAMPLE POSTURES LIST

1. "Everybody hates me" look
2. "I am better than you" look
3. "I just got a raise" look
4. "I am not valuable" look
5. "I deserve more respect" look
6. "I have too much to do" look
7. "I am jealous" look
8. "Oh what a beautiful morning" look
9. "TGIF (Thank God It's Friday)" look
10. "I like myself and I like you" look

Thought to Thought

Activity Summary

This exercise asks the participants, working from designated words, to let their thoughts flow and to record their free associations. This icebreaker is effective at any time during the learning program.

Training Application

Time Reference: Approximately 15 to 20 minutes.

Group Size: Best suited for a group of 10 to 20 participants.

Space Required: A room that is large enough to accommodate the comfortable seating of the participants.

Materials Needed: For each participant, a pencil and a piece of paper; for the trainer, a list of words to initiate the participants' thought processes (see Thought Starters List on the last page of this exercise).

Trainer Administration

1. While giving each participant a pencil and a piece of paper, the trainer explains that in this exercise the group members will be given words and asked to write down the objects, ideas, persons, animals, etc. that each word brings to mind. The trainer may wish to stress that this activity is merely an exercise and not a psychological test.

2. The group leader further explains that when a word is given (see Thought Starters List), the participants are to write down the word and then the next word, and the next word, and the next word, etc. that the initial word brings to mind. For example: If the word is "dog," the participant may write down "pet," then "bone," then "bite," then "Bowser," then "friend," etc., or the participant may be reminded of an entire scene from his or her past or from something he or she has read or seen.

3. After explaining the directions, the trainer reads a word from the Thought Starters List and allows the group members two minutes in which to record their thoughts.

4. The group leader then reads another word and so on until the participants have free-associated four or five words.

5. When the participants have recorded their reactions to the last word they are given, the trainer asks the group members to share some of their associations with the group and, if they can, to explain what triggered their choices and arrangements of particular words.
6. The group leader may conclude the activity with a discussion on the ways in which people arrange their thoughts and the impact of such patterns on their professional activities.

Variations

■ If the group contains more than 20 participants, the group leader may ask the participants to pair off and then perform step #5 in the Trainer Administration section with their partners.

■ The trainer may lead the group in free thought by writing a word on a blackboard or on a piece of newsprint taped to the wall. The group leader then records the word associations that the participants call out.

Trainer's Notes

_____

_____

_____

_____

_____

_____

_____

_____

THOUGHT STARTERS LIST

1. Work	6. Fire
2. Family	7. Water
3. School	8. Ice
4. Leisure	9. Fear
5. Earth	10. Love

Trust Me

This exercise asks the participants, wearing blind-folds, to trust their partners to lead them safely on a trust walk. This directed experience, generally more effective when used during the later stage of the training, is most appropriate for educational programs or sessions that emphasize personal inter-action among group members.

Time Reference: Approximately 15 to 20 minutes.
Group Size: Unlimited, but best suited for a group of 10 or more participants.
Space Required: A room that is large enough to permit the unrestricted movement of the learners.
Materials Needed: For each pair, a blindfold.

1. The trainer begins by explaining that in this ex-ercise each participant will be asked to trust an-other group member.
2. The participants are then instructed to pair off, each of them finding a partner that he or she feels is trustworthy.
3. Next the trainer gives each pair a blindfold. One of the partners puts on the blindfold in such a way that his or her vision is totally obstructed.
4. Without talking, each sighted partner then takes his or her blindfolded partner for a walk around the room. The sighted partner guides the blind-folded one in touching various objects, such as tables, the floor, a blackboard, other group mem-bers, a door, a wastebasket, etc. (The sighted part-ner may even take his or her partner outside of the room and into a new environment.)
5. After five minutes, the partners change roles, the sighted partner becoming the blindfolded one and vice versa. Again without talking, the partners take another five-minute trust walk.
6. When the allotted time has elapsed, the trainer reassembles the group and initiates a discussion on the feelings the participants experienced while they were the sighted and then the blindfolded partner.

Variations

■ The group leader may create an obstacle course through which the sighted partner must lead the blindfolded one.

■ The trainer may ask both partners to wear blindfolds. Without talking, the partners link arms and explore the room together.

Trainer's Notes

_____

_____

_____

_____

_____

_____

_____

_____

Warm Fuzzies

Activity Summary

This exercise asks the participants to share positive impressions and/or perceptions with one another. This directed experience is best implemented after the participants have had some opportunity to engage in feedback and disclosure during the learning program.

Training Application

Time Reference: Approximately 25 to 30 minutes.

Group Size: Unlimited, but best suited for a group of 10 to 20 participants. If the group contains more than 20 participants, subgroups should be formed.

Space Required: A room that has the potential for flexible seating.

Materials Needed: None.

Trainer Administration

1. The trainer asks the group members to form a circular seating arrangement.
2. When the participants are seated, the group leader explains that the participants will be exchanging "warm fuzzies" with one another. Warm fuzzies are positive statements that one makes or positive acts that one performs with no expectation of receiving something in return. Before proceeding with the activity, the trainer may ask that the group members give examples of what they consider to be "warm fuzzies."
3. Next the trainer asks for a volunteer to sit in the middle of the circle. If the group members appear overly anxious or inhibited, the trainer may consider serving as the first volunteer.
4. One at a time the participants compliment the volunteer by commenting on something they like, admire, or appreciate about the person. The volunteer is not to respond.
5. After all of the participants have given compliments, the volunteer returns to the circle, and a new volunteer comes forward to sit in the middle of the circle and receive compliments from his or her fellow group members. This process is repeated until all of the group members have had the opportunity to receive "warm fuzzies."
6. The trainer may process the activity by asking the

participants to comment briefly on their reactions to this experience.

Variations
■ The trainer can tell the volunteer to respond to the "warm fuzzies" as he or she sees fit.

■ The group leader can suggest that the participants not only give the volunteer "warm fuzzies" but that they each also mention one of the volunteer' characteristics that they would like to possess.

Trainer's Notes

_____

_____

_____

_____

_____

_____

_____

What I Believe

This exercise asks participants to respond to a series of statements about beliefs. This icebreaker is effective at any time during the learning program.

Time Reference: Approximately 15 to 20 minutes.

Group Size: Unlimited, but best suited for a group of 10 to 20 participants.

Space Required: An unobstructed area without tables or chairs.

Materials Needed: Trainer-prepared signs stating "Strongly Agree," "Mildly Agree," "Mildly Disagree," "Strongly Disagree," and "No Opinion"; and one copy of the Belief Statements List (see the last page of this exercise).

1. The trainer explains that the participants will be examining some statements and responding to them according to their personal beliefs.
2. The group leader then tapes the prepared signs up in various locations around the room.
3. The trainer then reads the first item on the Belief Statements List and then asks the participants to move over to and then stand beneath the sign that best represents their opinion; "Strongly Agree," "Mildly Agree," "Mildly Disagree," "Strongly Disagree," and "No Opinion."
4. When the participants are all standing beneath their chosen signs, the group leader reads the second statement on the list, and the participants each move to the sign that expresses their opinion. The procedure is repeated for all of the items on the Belief Statements List.
5. When the exercise has been completed, the participants discuss their reactions to the activity and to any of the items on the Belief Statements List.

■ The trainer may formulate a Belief Statements List that reflects work-related issues.
■ The group leader may choose statements that reflect the issues inherent in the particular training program. For example: statements on stress for a stress management workshop or statements on assertiveness for a supervision training program.

**Trainer's
Notes**

_____

_____

_____

_____

_____

_____

_____

_____

BELIEF STATEMENTS LIST

1. Welfare is misused by almost all of the people who are on it.
2. Women are equal to men in all respects.
3. There is only one true religion in the world.
4. Most politicians are on the take.
5. Juvenile delinquency is caused by environment.
6. Criminals are not made; they are born.
7. A four-day workweek is more efficient than a five-day workweek.
8. The press has the right to print whatever it wishes.
9. The federal government should subsidize amateur sports.
10. Every family should be limited to two children.

Who Am I Like?

Activity Summary This exercise asks the participants to compare themselves to famous persons. This activity is generally more effective when used in the early stage of the group's formation.

Training Application

Time Reference: Approximately 15 to 20 minutes.
Group Size: Unlimited.
Space Required: A room that contains adequate writing space for all of the participants.
Materials Needed: For each participant, a pencil and a piece of paper.

Trainer Administration

1. The trainer asks the group members to reflect upon themselves: their personalities, their backgrounds, their talents, their shortcomings, etc.
2. The trainer then requests that the participants each think of a famous person, living or deceased, with whom they feel they share certain similarities in personality, background, accomplishments, etc.
3. While the participants are gathering their thoughts, the trainer gives each group member a pencil and a piece of paper. The participants are then asked to write down the name of their chosen person and note how they are like the individual they have selected. For example: "I am like Eleanor Roosevelt because I am outspoken, not the greatest looker in the world, kind to others, well-educated, etc."
4. After five minutes, the trainer solicits a volunteer to share his or her reflections with the group. If the group members appear overly anxious or inhibited, the trainer may consider serving as the first volunteer.
5. The activity continues until all of the group members have had an opportunity to share their observations with the group.

Variations

■ The trainer may ask the participants to divide into groups of three or four. After sharing their reflections, the subgroup members take turns giving feedback about each member's selected person in light of their perceptions and/or impressions of that member.

■ The group leader may tell the participants that, if they wish, they may compare themselves to fictional characters.

_____

_____

_____

_____

_____

_____

_____

Whom Do You Trust?

Activity Summary

This exercise has the participants identify persons they trust and then examine the reasons for their trust. This structured experience is most appropriate for educational programs or sessions that emphasize personal interaction among group members. This activity is generally more effective when used in the early stage of the group's formation.

Training Application

Time Reference: Approximately 20 to 30 minutes.

Group Size: Unlimited.

Space Required: A room that contains adequate writing space for all of the participants.

Materials Needed: For each participant, a pencil and a piece of paper.

Trainer Administration

1. While giving each participant a pencil and a piece of paper, the trainer tells the group members that they will be identifying persons whom they trust and then explaining their reasons for trusting those particular individuals.
2. In a column on the left side of the piece of paper, each group member is to write the names of five individuals, in their personal or professional environment, whom he or she trusts totally (leaving an inch or two between each name).
3. Then, in a column running down the right side of the paper, each participant is to list next to each name he or she has written, his or her reason(s) for trusting that particular individual.
4. When the group members have finished this task, the trainer initiates a discussion in which the participants, based upon what they have written, share what the word "trust" means to them.
5. The group members conclude the exercise by brainstorming some of the ways in which trust can be developed among their fellow participants.

Variations

■ The trainer can use step #5 in the Trainer Administration section as the entire exercise. The group members brainstorm ways to build trust in a group or in their work environments.

■ The group leader may have the participants pair off to discuss ways in which trust can be fostered in their personal and/or professional settings.

Trainer's Notes

_____

_____

_____

_____

_____

_____

_____

_____

GAMES AND
BRAINTEASERS

Games and Brainteasers

Both enjoyable and exciting, games and brainteasers are effective vehicles for warming up the group members. This division contains a wide variety of materials that exercise the participants' physical and intellectual abilities.

Unfortunately, adults often believe that they should refrain from participating in activities that are viewed as "childish." Yet the "New Games" movement has demonstrated how much people of all ages crave the stimulation that comes from their participation in playful games. Although traditionally not considered training tools, games can heighten the impact of many learning programs. In addition to raising the energy level of the group, games can also function as introductory experiences to such important areas as problem solving, competition, team building, and consensus seeking. The receptiveness of group members to participating in a game will often depend upon such factors as the educational setting, the group members' comfort level, the group leader's attitude, and the icebreaker's content. More often than not, when participants feel that they have permission to engage in a game, they reduce their inhibitions and enjoy themselves greatly.

Brainteasers are more easily implemented because they are commonly viewed as "adult games." Focusing on the basic process of how we think, brainteasers are very flexible learning tools. In addition to breaking the ice between group members, these activities can also reduce learning overload when the material being presented becomes cumbersome or draining. Brainteasers can also nudge the participants' thought processes onto a different track; after all, shifting lanes in traffic may not get us to our destination any faster, but it does break the monotony.

The two types of icebreakers presented in this division provide the group leader with the ability to change the pace of the group dramatically. With a bit of encouragement, the participants may discover that they are able to recapture their capacity to see situations from new perspectives and/or to engage in spontaneous play.

Balloon Football

Activity Summary
This exercise is an energetic game in which the participants use balloons in playing a version of football. This activity is generally more effective when used during the later stage of the training program or session.

Training Application
Time Reference: Approximately 20 to 25 minutes.
Group Size: Best suited for a group of 20 or fewer participants.
Space Required: A large, unobstructed area without tables or chairs.
Materials Needed: Chalk or string, blue and red name tags or badges, and 30 balloons.

Trainer Administration
1. The trainer informs the participants that they will be playing balloon football, a modified version of the game played by Joe Namath, O. J. Simpson, and Fran Tarkenton.
2. The participants are asked to break into two teams, with an even number of participants on each team. Two or three volunteers are needed to serve as referees.
3. The group leader then gives one team blue name tags. The team members wear these badges and become the Blue Team. The members of the other team receive red badges and are known as the Red Team.
4. If necessary, the trainer asks the teams to clear the room in order to create a large area in which to play the game. Then the two teams blow up 30 balloons.
5. The trainer uses chalk or string to mark goal lines at each end of the room and to indicate the side boundaries of the playing field.
6. When the field has been cleared and the balloon footballs have been prepared, the trainer gathers the teams together and explains the rules of the game.
   a. The object of the game is for each team to put balloons over its own goal line.
   b. Each team divides itself into offensive and defensive players. The players on offense are responsible for batting the balloons past their

own goal line, while the players on defense are responsible for batting balloons away from the opposing team's goal line, thus keeping that team from scoring.

c. Before the game the members of each team's offense and defense position themselves on the playing field (see Diagram of Possible Player Positions).

d. A player may not move from the spot he or she has selected; however, he or she may stretch out or jump straight up in the air to reach a balloon.

e. To start the game, the trainer throws five balloons out into the middle of the playing field.

g. A player may pick a balloon off of the floor, but he or she must then immediately bat it into the air.

h. A player may not go out of bounds or reach in to bat a balloon out of the goal area.

i. A referee or the trainer replaces a broken balloon by throwing a new one into the middle of the playing field.

j. A referee or the trainer retrieves any balloon that goes out of bounds and puts it back in play by throwing it into the middle of the playing field.

k. A balloon must be in the air when it crosses the goal line.

l. A referee or the trainer awards goals. After a goal, the scoring balloon is declared dead, and a new balloon is then thrown into the middle of the playing field.

m. The game ends when 15 minutes have elapsed or when all of the balloons have been broken or have scored goals.

7. After explaining the rules, the trainer throws five balloons into the middle of the circle, and the game begins.

8. When all of the balloons have been broken or have scored goals—or when 15 minutes have elapsed—the team with more balloons piled up behind it goal line is declared the winner.

Diagram of Possible Player Positions

RO	BD	BO	RD	BO
BD	RO	RD	BO	RD
RO	BD	BO	RD	BO
BD	RO	RD	BO	RD

RED TEAM GOAL LINE   BLUE TEAM GOAL LINE

RO — Red Offense   RD — Red Defense
BO — Blue Offense   BD — Blue Defense

Variations

■ The trainer may ask that each participant play the game with one hand only and hold the other hand behind his or her back.

■ The group leader may blindfold the players on offense; that team's defensive players must then give directions verbally to guide the offensive players in making their shots.

■ The trainer may have the participants use ping-pong balls instead of balloons. The team members blow the balls across the floor and play the game according to rules the trainer has adapted from those presented in the Trainer Administration section.

■ If the group contains more than 20 participants, the trainer may throw 10 or more balloons into the playing field. The game ends when all 50 balloons have been broken or have scored goals—or when 20 minutes have elapsed.

Trainer's Notes

_____

_____

_____

_____

_____

_____

_____

_____

Basket

This exercise asks the participants to create words that begin and end with specific letters. This icebreaker is effective at any time during the learning program .

Time Reference: Approximately 10 to 15 minutes.
Group Size: Unlimited.
Space Required: A room that contains adequate writing space for all of the participants. The area must be large enough to accommodate the comfortable seating of the group members.
Materials Needed: For each participant, a pencil and a trainer-prepared piece of paper with the word "basket" written on it in both correct and reverse orders.

1. The trainer gives each participant a pencil and a piece of paper with the word "basket" written on it in both correct and reverse orders.

B	T
A	E
S	K
K	S
E	A
T	B

2. The group leader then explains that the participants are to form words that begin and end with the letters that are across from each other. For example: The first letters across are "B" and "T" so a word might be "BeeT." The longer the word, the better. For example: "BeeT" is better than "BaT."
3. When the group members have all formed words from each of the letter combinations across, the trainer solicits a volunteer to share his or her list of words with the entire group.
4. The exercise continues until all of the participants have shared their words.
5. The participant who uses the most letters in creating his or her words is declared the winner.

Variations ■ The trainer may request that the participants form pairs. The partners then compete against each other, with one point awarded to the person who forms the longest word for each letter.
■ The group leader may divide the participants into two teams that are to compete against each other to form the longest word for each letter combination.

Trainer's Notes

_____

_____

_____

_____

_____

_____

_____

_____

Blown Out of Proportion

Activity Summary This exercise is a game in which the participants blow up balloons and then have a contest to see whose balloon goes the farthest when the air in it is released. This icebreaker is effective at any time during the learning program.

Training Application *Time Reference:* Approximately 5 minutes.
Group Size: Unlimited.
Space Required: An unobstructed area without tables or chairs. The room must be large enough to permit the unrestricted movement of the learners.
Materials Needed: For each participant, a balloon. (Extra balloons are needed to replace any that break.)

Trainer Administration
1. The group leader begins by asking the participants to line up along a designated starting line.
2. The trainer then gives each participant a balloon and explains that in this exercise the group members will be blowing up and then releasing their balloons.
3. Next each participant is instructed to blow his or her balloon up as fully as possible and then to hold the end tightly so that no air escapes.
4. The trainer explains that when he or she says "Go," all of the participants are to release their balloons. The group member whose balloon goes the farthest in front of the line wins the game.
5. The group leader says "Ready, set . . . go," the balloons are released, and the race is on.
6. The exercise concludes with the winner being crowned "Balloonist for the Day."

Variations
■ The trainer may divide the participants into two teams. Representatives from each team come forward to compete against each other, the winner of each confrontation receiving a point for his or her team. After all of the participants have competed, the team with the higher score is the winner.
■ The group leader may establish a finish line approximately 30 feet from the designated starting line. The participants line up along the starting line and blow up their balloons. At a signal from the trainer, all of the group members release their

balloons. Each participant must follow his or her balloon to the spot where it lands. Then he or she must blow the balloon up again, release it, and follow it to its landing place, repeating this task until the balloon crosses the finish line. The participant whose balloon crosses the finish line first is declared the winner.

Trainer's Notes

_____

_____

_____

_____

_____

_____

_____

_____

Buzzing Out!

Activity Summary

This exercise asks the participants to use the number 4 to play a well-known game called Buzz. This icebreaker is effective at any time during the learning program.

Training Application

Time Reference: Approximately 10 to 15 minutes.
Group Size: Best suited for a group of 20 or fewer participants.
Space Required: A room that has the potential for flexible seating.
Materials Needed: None.

Trainer Administration

1. The trainer first asks the group members to form a circular seating arrangement.
2. When the participants are seated, the group leader tells them that they are going to play Buzz, a well-known circle game. The group members are then asked to think of the number 4, numbers that contain 4, and numbers that are multiples of 4. For example: 4, 8, 12, and 14.
3. The trainer solicits a volunteer to serve as the head of the circle and then explains the rules of the game.
   a. The volunteer is to begin the exercise by saying "1"; the player to his or her right counts "2" and so on around the circle.
   b. However, when the counting reaches a number that contains a 4, the player whose turn it is must replace the 4 with the word "buzz." For example: The number 4 is "buzz," 14 is "buzz teen," and 24 is "twenty buzz."
   c. When the counting reaches a number that contains a multiple of 4, the player whose turn it is must say "buzz" for that multiple. For example: The number 8 becomes "buzz," as do the numbers 12 and 16.
   d. After a "buzz," the next group member continues the counting. For example: 3, buzz, 5, 6, 7, buzz, 9, etc.
   e. The counting must proceed as quickly as possible.
   f. If a player does not insert "buzz" for a number containing 4 or for a number that is a multiple

of 4, or if a player inserts a "buzz" where it does not belong, he or she must leave the circle.

g. After an error has been made, the next participant starts the counting with the next number. For example: If a player failed to say "thirty buzz" for 34, the next player starts the game with 35.

h. The game continues until only one player, the winner, remains.

4. After explaining the rules, the trainer asks the volunteer to begin the counting.

5. The exercise continues for 10 minutes.

Variations

■ The trainer may ask the group members to use some other number, such as 3 or 6; the number 2 is the most difficult.

■ The trainer may substitute another word for "buzz." For example: "ding," "pop," or "bong."

Trainer's Notes

_____

_____

_____

_____

_____

_____

_____

_____

Cake Walk

Activity Summary

This exercise asks the participants, working in teams, to solve various riddles. This icebreaker is effective at any time during the learning program.

Training Application

Time Reference: Approximately 5 to 10 minutes.

Group Size: Best suited for a group of 10 to 20 participants.

Space Required: A room that has the potential for flexible seating.

Materials Needed: For each team, a pencil and a copy of the Cake Riddles List (see the last page of this exercise).

Trainer Administration

1. The trainer first asks the participants to divide into two teams. The teams then sit in different areas of the room. Next each team chooses a team member who will serve as the group's representative.

2. While giving each team representative a pencil and a copy of the Cake Riddles List, the group leader explains that the two teams will be competing against each other to solve the series of riddles.

3. The teams are then given 10 minutes in which to record their answers to the riddles.

4. When the allotted time has elapsed, the two teams share their answers with one another. If any of the riddles were not solved or were solved incorrectly, the trainer reads the correct answers to the group.

5. The team that is the first to solve all of the riddles correctly, or that has more correct answers at the end of the allotted time, is declared the winner.

Variations

■ The trainer may ask the participants to work individually or in pairs to solve the cake riddles.

■ The group leader may divide the participants into two teams. Next the teams each create 10 riddles around a specific subject, such as flowers, birds, colors, etc. Then the teams spend 10 minutes solving each other's riddles.

Trainer's Notes

_____

_____

_____

_____

_____

_____

_____

_____

CAKE RIDDLES LIST

1. What would a cake for Gabriel be called?
2. What would a cake baked by Anita Bryant be called?
3. What would a cake baked by a geologist be called?
4. What would a cake baked for a sculptor be called?
5. What would a cake for little Jack Horner be called?
6. What would a cake for a monkey be called?
7. What would a cake for a weight watcher be called?
8. What would a cake baked for someone who lives off another person's generosity be called?
9. What would a cake baked for a gossip be called?
10. What would a cake for the baseball batter who sacrificed himself be called?

NSWERS

1. *angelfood cake*
2. *orange cake*
3. *layer cake*
4. *marble cake*
5. *plum cake*

6. *banana (or coconut) cake*
7. *pound cake*
8. *sponge cake*
9. *spice cake*
10. *bundt (bunt) cake*

Creative Refrigerators

Activity Summary

This exercise challenges the participants, working in small groups, to brainstorm creative uses for old refrigerators. This icebreaker is effective at any time during the learning program.

Training Application

Time Reference: Approximately 15 to 20 minutes.

Group Size: Best suited for a group of 12 to 20 participants.

Space Required: A room that has the potential for flexible seating. Several small meeting rooms or areas that provide private or semiprivate interaction are also needed.

Materials Needed: For each work group, a sheet of newsprint and a black marker.

Trainer Administration

1. The trainer informs the group members that they are going to take part in an activity that will challenge their ability to think quickly and creatively.
2. Next the group leader divides the participants into small work groups of four or five members each and gives each work group a sheet of newsprint and a black marker.
3. The group leader then explains that each work group is to brainstorm as many possible uses, reuses, etc. for junk refrigerators and to list these uses on the piece of newsprint. Any part of the appliance can be used; more than one junk refrigerator can be applied to a use. The trainer tells the work groups that they are to think and write as quickly as they can and that they are to let their imaginations run wild as they formulate their lists. For example: Use 1,000 junk refrigerators to make a miniature Wall of China and charge admission to make money to buy more used refrigerators; set the grilled shelves of one refrigerator on the edges of the fruit and vegetable bins and make a barbeque pit.
4. After telling the groups that they have 10 minutes in which to complete their task, the trainer instructs each work group to locate an area in which its members can work together with some degree of privacy. The work groups then prepare their lists.

5. When the allotted time has elapsed, the trainer calls the groups together. A volunteer from each work group then reads his or her group's list out loud to the entire group.
6. The work group with the longest (or most creative) list of uses, reuses, etc. for junk refrigerators is declared the winner.

Variations

■ The trainer may ask the work groups to brainstorm uses, reuses, etc. for other items, such as three-legged chairs , dried-up markers, etc.

■ The group leader may conduct the exercise as a group activity in which all of the participants brainstorm together, while the leader lists their ideas on newsprint taped to a wall.

Trainer's Notes

Entrance Exams

Activity
Summary This exercise asks the participants to think creatively as they attempt to solve a series of visual riddles. This icebreaker is effective at any time during the learning program.

**Training
Application** *Time Reference:* Approximately 5 to 10 minutes.
Group Size: Unlimited.
Space Required: A room that is large enough to accommodate the comfortable seating of the participants.
Materials Needed: For the trainer, a blackboard or a pad of newsprint, chalk or a black marker, and the Riddles List (see the last page of this exercise).

**Trainer
Administration** 1. The trainer explains that in this exercise the participants will be asked to think creatively to solve a series of visual riddles.
2. The group leader then tells the participants that they will be shown a series of diagrams (see Riddles List) one at a time and that they will have three minutes to determine what each diagram means. The group members may ask any questions they wish, but the trainer can only answer "yes" or "no".
3. The trainer draws the first diagram on the blackboard or newsprint, and the group members begin asking questions.
4. After three minutes or when the correct answer has been guessed, the group leader draws the second diagram. This process continues until the participants have viewed and then attempted to decipher all of the visual riddles.
5. The trainer may process the activity through a discussion on the elements of creative thinking, primarily the ability to view a situation from a different or new perspective.

Variations ■ The trainer may instruct the participants to work individually to solve the riddles.
■ The trainer may ask the participants to devise their own visual riddles for the rest of the group members to solve.

Trainer's Notes

_____

_____

_____

_____

_____

_____

_____

_____

RIDDLES LIST

1.
$$\frac{O}{\text{Ph.D. M.A. B.S.}}$$

1. $\dfrac{\text{O}}{\begin{array}{l}\text{Ph.D.}\\ \text{M.A.}\\ \text{B.S.}\end{array}}$

2.
O L B
U S E

3.
LE
VEL

4.
J
YOU U ME
S
T

5.
W
O
R
H
T

6.
T
O
W
N

7.
R
E
T
T
A
B

8. HE'S HIMSELF

9.
$$\frac{\text{CRAZY}}{\text{YOU}}$$

10.
$$\frac{\text{OATH}}{\text{UR}}$$

Fancy Sayings

This exercise challenges the participants to interpret written communication. This icebreaker is effective at any time during the learning program.

**Training
Application**

Time Reference: Approximately 10 to 15 minutes.

Group Size: Unlimited.

Space Required: A room that is large enough to accommodate the comfortable seating of the participants.

Materials Needed: For each participant, a pencil and a copy of the Fancy Sayings Sheet (see the last page of this exercise).

**Trainer
Administration**

1. The group leader gives each participant a pencil and a copy of the Fancy Sayings Sheet and tells the group members that they are not to look at the sayings until they are instructed to do so.

2. The trainer then explains that the group members will be taking part in an exercise that will challenge them to sort the simple from the obscure. Their task is to "decode" the famous sayings and slogans that have been obscured by "fancy" language. They will have 10 minutes to complete this task.

3. At a signal from the group leader, the participants work individually to decipher the well-known phrases or sayings. The participant who finishes first or who decodes the most sayings within the allotted time is declared the winner .

4. The trainer may then process the activity through a group discussion that focuses on the thought processes the participants used in decoding the sayings and slogans.

Variations

■ The trainer can ask the group members to work together to decode the sayings.

■ The group leader can request that the participants, working individually, choose well-known slogans and mask them in "fancy" language. (A number of dictionaries may be needed for reference.) Each group member then reads his fancy saying out loud, and the entire group attempts to decode it.

■ The trainer can divide the group into two teams. The teams have 10 minutes in which to create at least five fancy sayings to present to the other team. (Several dictionaries may be needed for reference.) Each saying is to be written on a separate sheet of paper. After 10 minutes the teams take turns decoding one another's fancy saying. If a team decodes a saying within 30 seconds, one point is awarded. When all of the fancy sayings have been decoded or when the time limit has expired, the team with the higher score is declared the winner.

Trainer's Notes

_____

_____

_____

_____

_____

_____

_____

FANCY SAYINGS SHEET

1. A feathered vertebrate enclosed in the grasping organ has an estimated worth that is higher than a duo encapsulated in the branched shrub.

2. It is sufficiently more tolerable to bestow upon than to come into possession.

3. The medium of exchange is the origin or source of the whole amount of sorrow, distress, and calamity.

4. A monetary unit equal to 1/100 of a pound that is stored aside is a monetary unit equal to 1/100 of a pound that is brought in by way of returns.

ANSWERS

1. *A bird in the hand is worth two in the bush.*
2. *It is better to give than to receive.*
3. *Money is the root of all evil.*
4. *A penny saved is a penny earned.*

Grab Your Partner

Activity Summary This exercise asks the participants to pair off and then, marching in different circles, to locate their partners faster than other pairs. This icebreaker is effective at any time during the learning program.

Training Application

Time Reference: Approximately 10 to 15 minutes.

Group Size: Best suited for a group of 14 or more participants.

Space Required: An unobstructed area without tables or chairs.

Materials Needed: A record player and records, or a tape recorder and tapes. (Marches with quick tempos are most appropriate for this activity.)

Trainer Administration

1. The trainer first asks the participants to pair off. If the group is uneven in number, the person without a partner becomes a referee.
2. Next the participants are to form two circles, one inside the other. One partner is to be in the outer circle, while the other partner is to be part of the inner circle.
3. The group leader explains that when the music begins, the members of the outer circle are to march clockwise around their circle, while the participants in the inner circle march counter-clockwise around their circle. When the trainer stops the music, the partners are to go to one another, touch shoulders, and squat down. The last partners to locate each other and to squat are out of the game and will help referee the next rounds.
4. After explaining the game, the trainer starts the music, and the game begins.
5. The exercise continues until only one pair, the winner, remains.

Variations

■ The group leader may vary the tempo of the music, with the participants speeding up or slowing down their marching accordingly.

■ If the group is very large, the trainer may have the participants form groups of three members each. (At least three volunteers are needed to serve as referees.) The participants march in three circles, the outer circle moving clockwise, the middle circle counterclockwise, and the inner circle clockwise. The exercise then follows the basic procedure outlined in the Trainer Administration section.

Trainer's Notes

_____

_____

_____

_____

_____

_____

_____

_____

Hidden Birds

This exercise asks the participants to find birds' names that have been hidden in sentences. This ice-breaker is effective at any time during the learning program.

Time Reference: Approximately 5 to 10 minutes.
Group Size: Unlimited.
Space Required: A room that is large enough to accommodate the comfortable seating of the participants.
Materials Needed: For each participant, a pencil and a copy of the Hidden Birds List (see the last page of this exercise).

1. The trainer gives each group member a pencil and a copy of the Hidden Birds List.
2. The group leader then explains that the participants will be playing a game that requires sharp eyes. Buried in each of the sentences is the name of a bird. The letters of the birds' names appear in order in the sentences. However, bird names can be composed of letters in more than one word. For example: We have hig*h en*rollment (hen).
3. The participants are then given five minutes in which to find all of the hidden birds that they can.
4. When the allotted time has elapsed, the participant who has discovered the most birds in the least amount of time is declared the winner.

■ The trainer may create sentences that contain hidden flowers, trees, or animals.
■ The group leader may ask each participant to create hidden-word sentences to share with the rest of the group.

_____

_____

_____

_____

_____

HIDDEN BIRDS LIST

1. Carol's microwave oven has four settings.
2. Now, let me help you with your coat.
3. She can recognize a gleam in his eye.
4. That particular kind of dessert is superb.
5. Did you see that the pigs wallowed in the mud out back?
6. Marilyn, the movie star, lingered on the stage.
7. No, I just saw her on the bus.
8. The February thaw killed the crop.
9. The throb in my arm is caused by a cramp.
10. The kids want to leave early.

ANSWERS

1. crow	*6. starling*
2. owl	*7. heron*
3. eagle	*8. hawk*
4. lark	*9. robin*
5. swallow	*10. swan*

Hiding Spot

Activity Summary This exercise tests the participants' abilities to observe their environment closely and carefully as they search for small objects the trainer has hidden in the room. This icebreaker is effective at any time during the learning program.

Training Application *Time Reference:* Approximately 15 to 20 minutes.
Group Size: Unlimited.
Space Required: A room that is large enough to permit the unrestricted movement of the learners.
Materials Needed: For each participant, a pencil and a piece of paper; 20 different small objects (button, safety pin, penny, straw, bottle cap, etc.) and a trainer-prepared list of the objects and where each has been hidden in the room.

Trainer Administration

1. Before the participants arrive, the trainer places 20 different, small objects around the room in settings where they do not ordinarily belong. For example: a button on a thermostat, a straw balanced on a light switch, etc. At this time the group leader compiles a list of the objects and their hiding places.

2. As the participants enter the room, the group leader gives each of them a pencil and a piece of paper and asks them to be seated.

3. When all of the group members are seated, the trainer explains that they will be participating in an activity that tests their powers of observation. They are going to locate small objects that have been placed in unusual locations around the room. (The trainer should give two or three hypothetical examples of objects and locations.)

4. Next the trainer tells the group members that they are to walk around the room and to try to locate these small objects. When they observe an item, they are, without touching the object or signaling others as to its whereabouts, to write the name of the object and describe where they have found it.

5. After explaining the exercise, the group leader tells the participants to stand and begin their search.

6. After 15 minutes the trainer asks the group member to return to their seats. When the participants are seated, the group leader asks who found all of the objects, who found 19 objects, who found 18, who found 17, etc., until the person who has found the most objects has been identified.
7. The group leader then reads the list of objects, and the participants reveal the location of each item on the list.

Variations
■ The trainer may tell the group members the total number of the objects that have been hidden in the room.
■ The group leader may ask the participants to work in pairs to find the hidden items.

Trainer's Notes

_____

_____

_____

_____

_____

_____

_____

_____

_____

Hot-Air Specialist

Activity Summary

This exercise asks the participants, working in teams, to compete against one another in a relay involving facial tissue, straws, and their own hot air. This activity is generally more effective when used during the later stage of the training program or session.

Training Application

Time Reference: Approximately 10 to 15 minutes.

Group Size: Unlimited, but best suited for a group of 20 or fewer participants.

Space Required: An unobstructed area without tables or chairs. The room must be large enough to permit the unrestricted movement of the learners.

Materials Needed: Facial tissue and, for each participant, a straw.

Trainer Administration

1. The trainer holds up a straw and a piece of facial tissue and tells the participants that these are the materials they will use in a relay race.

2. The participants are then instructed to stand and to divide into two teams, with an equal number of participants on each team. Next the teams are to form two parallel lines with the members of one team facing the members of the other team. (If the group contains an uneven number, one participant can serve as a referee.)

3. When the lines have formed, the trainer gives each participant a straw and explains that the object of the game is to suck the tissue into the end of the straw and to pass the tissue to the next person in line who must then suck the tissue into his or her straw. (No hands can be used.) If the tissue drops to the floor, the team member who is to receive it must, without using his or her hands, suck the tissue off of the floor.

4. The group leader then hands a tissue to the first person in each team's line. At a signal from the trainer, the game begins.

5. The exercise continues until all of the team members in each line have had an opportunity to receive and pass the tissue.

6. The members of the team that finishes first are declared the "Hot-Air Specialists."

■ The trainer may ask the teams to place their chairs in two rows and to complete the exercise while sitting down.

■ The group leader may have each team compete against the clock. The first team passes the tissue while the members of the second team try, without touching the participants, to distract them. For example: One team plays while members of the other team jump up and down, make funny faces, and wave their hands in the players' faces. When the members of the second team play, the members of the first team attempt to distract them. The team with the lower time score is declared the winner.

Trainer's Notes

_____

_____

_____

_____

_____

_____

_____

_____

Jigsaw Puzzle

This exercise asks the participants to work with other group members to complete a jigsaw puzzle. This icebreaker is effective at any time during the learning program.

Time Reference: Approximately 10 to 15 minutes.

Group Size: Unlimited, but best suited for a group of 12 to 20 participants.

Space Required: A large, unobstructed area offering adequate work space for each work group.

Materials Needed: For each work group, a cut-up copy of the Jigsaw Puzzle (see the last page of this exercise).

1. After informing the group members that they will be competing in an exercise that requires team work, the trainer asks the participants to divide into work groups of four or five members each. The groups are then to spread out around the room so that each of them has some privacy in which to work.

2. Next the trainer asks a representative from each work group to come forward and receive the pieces of his or her group's puzzle. The representatives then return to their respective groups and distribute the pieces of the puzzle to the work group members. The trainer emphasizes that the groups are not to begin assembling the puzzle until they are instructed to do so.

3. When the participants all have their puzzle pieces, the trainer tells the groups to begin putting the pieces together to form a square.

4. The activity continues until all of the work groups have completed their puzzles. The group to put the jigsaw puzzle together first is declared the winner.

■ The group leader may instruct the members of each work group to wear blindfolds while they attempt to complete their puzzle.

■ The trainer may ask each work group to construct a puzzle (containing no more than eight pieces) for another group to complete. (Poster board is recommended for the puzzles.) The work groups then exchange puzzles. The first group to complete its puzzle is declared the winner.

Trainer's Notes

_____

_____

_____

_____

_____

_____

_____

_____

JIGSAW PUZZLE

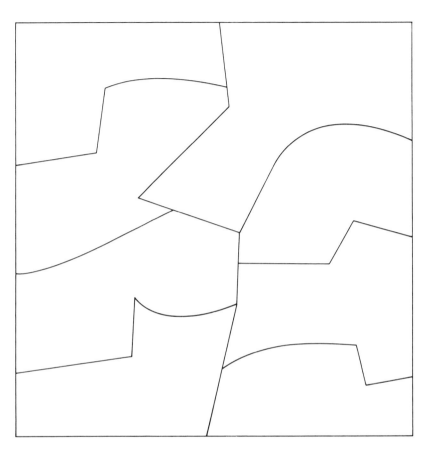

Mule Train

Activity Summary This exercise is a relay race in which the participants compete as mule teams to complete an obstacle course. This activity is generally more effective when used during the later stage of the training program or session.

Training Application

Time Reference: Approximately 15 to 20 minutes.

Group Size: Unlimited, but best suited for a group of 12 or more participants.

Space Required: An unobstructed area without tables or chairs.

Materials Needed: For each team, six chairs, two blindfolds, and one five-foot length of heavy-duty string with two loops tied in it (see Diagram of Harness and Course).

Trainer Administration

1. The trainer begins the activity by explaining that the participants will be involved in a relay race in which they will form mule teams.

2. The group members are to divide into two teams, and each team is then to line up behind an imaginary starting line.

3. While the teams line up, the trainer creates a race course for one team, placing six chairs in a zigzag pattern across the floor (see Diagram of Harness and Course); an identical obstacle course is then made for the second team.

4. Next the group leader explains the rules of the game.

   a. Three members of each team form a mule team, two serving as mules and one becoming the driver.

   b. The mules put on blindfolds, and the driver attaches the string around the mules' waists (see Diagram of Harness and Course).

   c. At a signal from the trainer, the driver from each team, pulling on the strings to guide the mules, must then guide his or her mule team through the obstacle course (Note: The trainer should caution the group members not to be overly zealous, for the mules might collide or fall. Avoid injury!)

d. In each confrontation, the mule team to complete the obstacle course first, without knocking over any of the chairs (or while moving the fewer number of chairs) receives one point for its team.

e. When the mule teams have completed the course, the mules remove their blindfolds and harnesses; the drivers and mules then quickly return to their respective teams.

f. After the next two mule teams are blindfolded and hitched up, the drivers guide them through their respective courses; a point is again awarded to the winning team.

g. If only one or two team members remain at the end of a team's line, a player or two players who have already competed may become part of this last team.

5. After explaining the rules and allowing some time for the first mule teams from each team to ready themselves, the trainer says "Move 'em out!" and the game begins.

6. The exercise continues until all of the mule teams have completed the course.

7. The team with the higher number of points is declared the winner.

Diagram of Harness and Course

HARNESS

String Around Waist

COURSE

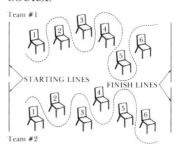

Team #1

STARTING LINES   FINISH LINES

Team #2

Variations ■ The trainer may make the game more difficult by having each team use mule teams that have four mules and two drivers. To form a larger mule team, the members of each mule team link arms. The drivers must work together to guide the mules through the course.

■ The group leader may instruct mule teams from each team to cover the same obstacle course at the same time.

■ If the group is small, subgroups of three may compete against the clock. The subgroup with the lowest time is the winner.

■ If the group contains more than 30 participants, three or more teams may be formed.

Trainer's Notes

_____

_____

_____

_____

_____

_____

_____

_____

_____

Object Drop

Activity Summary This exercise asks the participants to use their sense of hearing to identify various objects. This icebreaker is effective at any time during the learning program.

Training Application

Time Reference: Approximately 10 to 15 minutes.
Group Size: Unlimited.
Space Required: A room that has the potential for flexible seating.
Materials Needed: For each participant, a pencil and a piece of paper; for the trainer, a small table (if the floor is carpeted) and a sack of objects (see the Items List on the last page of this exercise).

Trainer Administration

1. After distributing paper and pencils to all of the group members, the trainer explains that this exercise is designed to challenge their sense of hearing. The group leader then asks the participants to turn their chairs so that they are facing away from the front of the room.

2. As the group leader calls out a number and then drops each of the common objects (see Items List) on a hard surface (floor or table top), the participants are to write down the number of the object and then its identity based on the sound it makes when it is dropped on the floor or table. (The trainer may wish to drop the items one at a time again, in the same order, to assist the group members in identifying the objects.)

3. When all of the objects have been dropped, the trainer reviews the Items List with the group members to see how many of the objects they have identified correctly.

4. The trainer may process the exercise through a group discussion that focuses on the use of the five senses in daily communication and in problem solving.

Variations

■ The trainer may attempt to confuse the group members by dropping similar sounding objects in sequence. For example: a key, a coin, and a metal measuring spoon.

■ To make the participants concentrate harder and think more quickly, the group leader may speed up the dropping of the objects, allowing the participants only three seconds in which to identify each object that is dropped.

_____

_____

_____

_____

_____

_____

_____

_____

ITEMS LIST

1. Key
2. Rubber ball
3. Unopened can of food
4. Book
5. Frying pan
6. Pair of scissors
7. Pencil
8. Penny

9. Half-dollar
10. Orange
11. Ruler
12. Magazine
13. Shoe
14. Tablespoon
15. Metal ashtray
16. Piece of paper

Observation

Activity Summary

This exercise tests the participants' powers of observation when they are confronted by a strangely dressed visitor who comes into the room. This icebreaker is effective at any time during the learning program.

Training Application

Time Reference: Approximately 10 to 15 minutes.

Group Size: Unlimited.

Space Required: A room that contains adequate writing space for all of the participants. The area must be large enough to accommodate the comfortable seating of the group members.

Materials Needed: For each participant, a pencil and a piece of paper; a prearranged visit by an unusually dressed visitor and a trainer-prepared list of the clothing the visitor wears and the objects he or she carries .

Trainer Administration

1. Before the session the trainer must arrange for a person to enter the room, ask the group a question, and then leave. The visitor should be dressed strangely, wearing as many articles of clothing and pieces of jewelry as possible. The question the person asks may be "Excuse me, I am looking for _____."

2. As the trainer distributes paper and pencils to all of the group members, the visitor enters the room, poses the chosen question, remains for several seconds, and then leaves.

3. After the visitor has left the room, the group leader tells the participants that this exercise is designed to test their powers of observation. The participants are each to list everything they can remember about the visitor: the clothing and jewelry he or she wore, any objects he or she carried, the question he or she asked, etc.

4. After 10 minutes the group members, one at a time, read their lists out loud and then check their observation skills by comparing their lists to the trainer-prepared list describing the visitor and his or her attire.

5. The trainer may process the exercise through a

discussion on the importance of observation and differing perceptions.

Variations
■ The trainer and the visitor may carry on a predetermined conversation at the front of the room. When the visitor has left, two of the participants volunteer to recreate the scene they have just witnessed.
■ The group leader may arrange for two unusually dressed strangers to enter the room at the same time.

Trainer's Notes

_____

_____

_____

_____

_____

_____

_____

_____

Puzzlers

Activity Summary

This exercise asks the participants to examine the kinds of puzzles that they have always been unable to solve or have had difficulty solving. This icebreaker is effective at any time during the learning program.

Training Application

Time Reference: Approximately 25 to 30 minutes.
Group Size: Unlimited.
Space Required: A room that has the potential for flexible seating.
Materials Needed: None.

Trainer Administration

1. The trainer asks the group members to put on their thinking caps and to call to mind some riddle, puzzle, or trick that always "stumped" them when they were children.
2. The group leader then asks the participants to pair off and to discuss with their partners the kinds of puzzles or riddles that they find difficult to solve or to find answers for. They are also to examine any reasons they can discern for the difficulties they encounter in solving these kinds of "puzzlers." The partners then choose one of the puzzlers or riddles to share with the group.
3. One at a time, the pairs present their riddle or puzzle and request that the other group members give their answers or solutions. If, within three minutes, the group has not solved the puzzle, the partners give the correct answer.
4. The exercise continues until all of the pairs have presented their puzzlers.
5. The trainer then initiates a discussion of puzzlers, encouraging the group members to share their feelings about their own problem-solving skills.

Variation

■ The trainer may present several sample puzzlers, i.e., mathematical, logical, position, word, and trick puzzles or riddles. The group members use these examples as a basis for their discussion of the thought processes involved in problem solving.

_____

_____

_____

_____

_____

_____

_____

_____

_____

Rhythm

Activity Summary

This exercise is a rhythm game in which the participants name objects that fit into designated categories. This icebreaker is effective at any time during the learning program.

Training Application

Time Reference: Approximately 5 to 10 minutes.

Group Size: Unlimited, but best suited for a group of 20 or fewer participants.

Space Required: A room that has the potential for flexible seating.

Materials Needed: None.

Trainer Administration

1. The trainer asks the group members to form a circular seating arrangement.
2. When the participants are seated, the group leader explains that they will be playing a rhythm game in which they name objects that fit specific categories.
3. The trainer then demonstrates the rhythm portion of the game. The participants are to pat their knees two times with both hands, clap their hands twice, and then snap their fingers two times. The group members practice the rhythm together until they have established the tempo for the game.
4. After soliciting a volunteer to serve as the head of the circle, the group leader explains the rules of the game.
   a. On the snap portion of the rhythm, the volunteer is to name a category. For example: cars, food, colors, animals, rivers, state capitals, etc.
   b. The rhythm continues, and on the next snap the participant sitting to the right of the volunteer names an object that fits into the category. For example: If the category is food, the participant might say "broccoli."
   c. Then on the next snap the third person names another object, and so on around the circle.
   d. Objects may not be repeated for a category in any one round.
   e. If a participant cannot think of an object that fits the designated category, on the snap he or she may call out the word "category." On the

next snap, the person to the right must name a new category, and the game continues. (A category can only be changed once during a round.)

f. If a participant does not name an object or call out "category," then he or she leaves the circle, and the next player names a new category for the next round.

g. The game continues until only one participant remains or until five minutes have elapsed.

5. When all of the rules have been explained, the trainer begins the rhythm pattern, and the participant serving as the head of the circle calls out a category on the snap. (As the game progresses, the trainer may wish to speed up the tempo of the rhythm.)

6. After five minutes, the trainer stops the activity.

Variation

■ The trainer may begin the exercise by naming a word on the snap. On the next snap the participant sitting to the group leader's right must name a word that begins with the last letter of that word, and so forth around the circle. For example: The trainer calls out "ball," the next person says "love," the following person says "elephant," etc. If a participant fails to select a word at his or her snap, he or she leaves the circle, and the game continues with the next person calling out a word.

Trainer's Notes

_____

_____

_____

_____

_____

_____

_____

_____

Scrambled Cities

This exercise asks the participants to unscramble the
names of American cities. This icebreaker is effective
at any time during the learning program.

Time Reference: Approximately 10 to 15 minutes.
Group Size: Unlimited.
Space Required: A room that has the potential for flexible seating.
Materials Needed: For each participant, a pencil and
a copy of the Scrambled Cities List (see the last
page of this exercise).

1. The trainer begins by asking the participants to
form pairs. The partners are then to locate a space
in which they can work with some degree of privacy.
2. While distributing pencils and copies of the Scrambled Cities List to all of the participants, the trainer
explains that the pairs will be playing a game in
which they are to unscramble the names of American cities. The pair that unscrambles the names
first, or that unscrambles the most names within
10 minutes, will be declared the winner.
3. At a signal from the trainer the pairs begin working. After 10 minutes or when one pair has unscrambled all of the names, the trainer reads the
list of unscrambled cities.

■ The group leader may use the scrambled names
of states, countries, bodies of water, etc., or the
trainer may scramble words that relate to the topic
under study.
■ The trainer may divide the group members into
two teams of equal size. The teams then compete
against each other to see who can unscramble the
names first.

_____

_____

_____

Trainer's Notes
continued

_____

_____

_____

_____

_____

SCRAMBLED CITIES LIST

1. Cocigah
2. Sladal
3. Ysactaknis
4. Lybnaa
5. Ribolatem

6. Thanigsnow
7. Havnilles
8. Polaninesim
9. Noldpart
10. Kenwory

NSWERS

1. *Chicago*
2. *Dallas*
3. *Kansas City*
4. *Albany*
5. *Baltimore*

6. *Washington*
7. *Nashville*
8. *Minneapolis*
9. *Portland*
10. *New York*

Spell It Out

Activity Summary

This exercise is a game in which the participants, working in teams, compete against one another to spell out words. This icebreaker is effective at any time during the training program.

Training Application

Time Reference: Approximately 10 to 15 minutes.
Group Size: Best suited for a group of 15 to 25 participants.
Space Required: An unobstructed area without tables or chairs.
Materials Needed: For each participant, a paper plate with a letter of the alphabet printed on it; for the trainer, the preprepared Sample Word List (see the last page of this exercise). For small groups, each team member may receive two paper plates representing two different letters. To prepare for this exercise, the trainer needs to know the exact number of participants who will be in the group.

Trainer Administration

1. The trainer begins by explaining that this exercise asks the participants, working in teams, to spell out words.

2. The group leader then divides the participants into two teams, with an equal number of group members on each team. If the group contains an odd number of participants, one person may act as a referee.

3. The members of one team are instructed to stand together at one end of the room, while the members of the other team are to gather at the opposite end of the room.

4. Next the trainer gives the teams identical sets of paper plates with letters written on them. Each team member receives one plate. If the group is small, each team member may receive two plates with different letters written on them. (The trainer must be certain that both teams have the same set of letters and that the words that are to be spelled contain those letters.)

5. The group leader then explains that both teams will be asked to spell the same word at the same time. When the trainer calls out a word (see Sample Word List), the team members who have the

letters must run 10 feet out in front of their team, face their group, and position themselves to spell the word. The first team to spell the word correctly receives one point. If a letter is repeated twice, the team member with that letter must move back and forth between both positions of the letter. If a team member possesses two different letters that are both used in a word, he or she must move back and forth between both positions of the letters.

6. After explaining the rules, the trainer calls out the first word, and the game begins.

7. The game continues until one team has earned five points.

Variations

■ The trainer may add suspense to the game by calling out a sentence, the last word of which is the one to be spelled out. For example: "I went to a party and had a B-A-L-L."

■ The group leader may pose questions, and the teams must decide upon and then spell out the answers. For example: If the questions is "What bird is said to be wise?" the teams might spell out O-W-L.

Trainer's Notes

_____

_____

_____

_____

_____

_____

_____

_____

SAMPLE WORD LIST

1. Naive
2. Skier
3. Climb
4. Rhyme
5. Mantle
6. Upset

7. Thunder
8. Rebound
9. Pilot
10. Mishap
11. Justify
12. Ideal

Telephone Book Relay

Activity Summary

This exercise is a game in which the participants, working in teams, compete against each other to locate telephone numbers. This icebreaker is effective at any time during the learning program.

Training Application

Time Reference: Approximately 15 to 20 minutes.

Group Size: Unlimited, but best suited for a group of 12 or more participants.

Space Required: A room that has the potential for flexible seating.

Materials Needed: For each participant, a pencil and a piece of paper; for the trainer, two telephone directories for the same city, masking tape, a pre-prepared list of page, column, and line numbers printed on a large sheet of newsprint (see Sample Numbers List on the last page of this exercise), and an answer sheet showing the correct telephone number for each page-column-line combination.

Trainer Administration

1. After explaining that the group members will be playing a game that requires them to concentrate and to handle details quickly, the trainer divides the group members into two teams.
2. The teams are then directed to place their chairs in two rows four feet apart and to sit with the teams facing each other.
3. When the teams are seated, the group leader gives the first person in each row a telephone directory and then distributes paper and pencils to all of the participants.
4. Next the trainer explains the rules of the game:
   a. A sheet of newsprint will be taped to the floor or held by the trainer so that all of the group members can view its contents. On the newsprint are page numbers, column numbers, and line numbers from the directories in the possession of each team (see Sample Numbers List).
   b. At a signal from the trainer, the first person in each row looks at the first number combination written on the newsprint. He or she turns to the correct page number, scans the

correct column, locates the correct line number, and then writes down the telephone number on his or her piece of paper.

c. The person then passes the directory to the team member sitting next to him or her. The team member follows the page-column-line directions to locate the second telephone number, writes it down, and passes the directory to the next player, and so on until all of the phone numbers have been recorded.

d. If each team contains more than 10 participants, the trainer will need to add more page, column, and line numbers to the list (see Sample List of Numbers.)

e. If each team contains fewer than 10 participants, when the directories reach the end of each row, they are passed to the front of the row, and the players continue to work through the list until all of the numbers have been identified or until 15 minutes have elapsed.

f. The winner is the first team to identify correctly all of the numbers on the list or the team that correctly identifies more numbers within the 15-minute deadline.

5. After explaining the rules, the trainer gives a signal, and the first players in each row use the page column, and line directions to locate the first telephone number on the list.

6. The activity continues until both teams have completed the list or until 15 minutes have elapsed. Then, referring to his or her answer sheet of correct numbers, the trainer checks the answers of both teams and declares the winner of the game.

Variations
- The trainer can give each participant a director and instruct the group members to work through the list individually.

- Instead of using a written list, the group leader may call out the page, column, and line numbers. After allowing 30 seconds for the team member to find the correct number, the trainer calls out the next set of number directions. If, within that time, a player has not yet found the number, he or she must stop looking and pass the director to the next team member.

■ The trainer may direct the team members to list both the name and telephone number for each page-column-line combination.

Trainer's Notes

_____

_____

_____

_____

_____

_____

_____

_____

SAMPLE NUMBERS LIST

Page	Column	Line
110	2	26
50	1	5
35	3	16
40	1	12
52	2	10
75	3	8
64	3	7
47	3	2
32	2	4
17	1	25

Testing Your Logic

This exercise tests the participants' use of logic. This icebreaker is effective at any time during the learning program.

Training Application
Time Reference: Approximately 15 to 20 minutes.
Group Size: Unlimited, but best suited for a group of 10 to 16 participants. If the group contains more than 16 participants, additional work groups should be formed.
Space Required: A room that has the potential for flexible seating.
Materials Needed: For each participant, a pencil and a copy of the Puzzles Sheet (see the next to the last page of this exercise).

Trainer Administration
1. The group leader begins by explaining that the participants will be taking part in an exercise that is designed to challenge their reasoning powers.
2. After giving each participant a pencil and a copy of the Puzzle Sheet, the trainer tells the participants to divide into two work groups, with a balanced number of participants in each group. The members of each group are to work together to come up with an answer for each puzzle. They must also be able to explain how and why they arrived at each answer.
3. The work groups are then given 15 minutes in which to solve the puzzles.
4. When the allotted time has elapsed, the trainer asks for a volunteer from each group to explain the answer to the first problem. If the answers are partially or wholly incorrect, the trainer then reads the correct answer to the entire group.
5. A volunteer from each work group is solicited to answer the second puzzle, and the process is repeated until explanations have been given for all five problems.

Variations
■ The trainer may ask that the participants work individually to solve the problems.
■ The group leader may request that the participants divide into two groups, each group devising puzzles for the other group to solve.

■ The trainer may read each logic problem out loud and then have all of the group members work together to find an answer.

Trainer's Notes

_____

_____

_____

_____

_____

_____

_____

_____

PUZZLES SHEET

1. A customer in a restaurant ordered two cups of coffee and three doughnuts. He dunked one doughnut in one cup of coffee and two doughnuts in the other. Noticing his actions, the waitress said, "What are you doing there, sailor?" How did she know that he was a sailor?

2. A man buys five cigarettes each day. When he smokes a cigarette, he saves the butt; when he has five butts, he makes another cigarette from them. If he buys cigarettes for 25 days, how many will he be able to smoke?

3. Hank Bent, the old trapper, has been out on his trap line in northern Minnesota with the temperature at 50 degrees below zero. He is delayed by a blizzard and, almost frozen, is barely able to stumble into his shack. The shack is extremely cold, but a fire is laid in the stove, ready to be lit. Hank looks at the fireplace, at the old lamp filled with oil, at a candle in its holder, and then at the single match that stands between him and death by freezing. Which shall he light first?

4. Jim and Bill engaged in a rifle-shooting contest, comparing their success in hitting a small target from a considerable distance. They took 50 shots each and made the same number of hits, 25. After taking a break to get a drink, they resumed their contest. They did not shoot as well this time; Jim got only three hits in 34 shots, while Bill got no hits in 25 shots. Since Jim's record after their break was better than Bill's and since his record before the drink was just as good as Bill's, Jim's record for the day was clearly better than Bill's. Or was it?

5. There is something fishy about the following telephone conversation. What is it?

"Good morning, Jackson Fish Packing Firm."
"May I please talk with Mr. Jereld?"
"Who is calling, please?"
"This is George Edwards."
"I beg your pardon, but I did not catch the name."
"George Edwards. E for evangelical, D for diversification, W for waterproof, A for antagonistic . . ."
"Excuse me, sir, but A for what?"
"A for antagonistic, R for reprehensible, D for developmental, S for sacroiliac—Edwards."
"Thank you, sir. Mr. Jereld is ready to talk."

PUZZLES SHEET (continued)

ANSWERS

1. *The customer was wearing a sailor suit.*
2. *In 25 days the man will buy 125 cigarettes. From the butts of the 125 he will make 25 cigarettes; from the butts of the 25 he will make five; and from the butts of the five cigarettes he will make one cigarette. Altogether he will have 156 cigarettes.*
3. *Hank will first light the match.*
4. *No, Jim's record was not better than Bill's but just equal to it. The only proper way to measure the marksmanship is by the ratio of hits to attempts. Jim's rating was 28/84 and Bill's was 25/75; therefore, they tied with a rating of 0.333.*
5. *The point is that the question "A for what?" would not be asked since the listener already knew that the letter in question was "A."*

The Fifth Sense

Activity Summary

This exercise challenges the participants to use their sense of touch to identify specific objects. This icebreaker is effective at any time during the training program.

Training Application

Time Reference: Approximately 15 to 20 minutes.

Group Size: Best suited for a group of 10 to 20 participants.

Space Required: A room that contains adequate writing space for all of the participants.

Materials Needed: For each participant, a blindfold, a pencil, and a piece of paper; for the trainer, a table, a tablecloth, and a variety of simple, yet interesting household objects (skein of yarn, orange, stapler, note pad, sponge, lightbulb, beer can, mophead, plastic bag, bar of soap, etc.).

Trainer Administration

1. Before the participants arrive, the trainer needs to place a variety of simple, yet interesting household objects on a table and then cover the table with a piece of cloth.

2. When the participants have entered the room and seated themselves, the trainer explains that they will be taking part in an activity that is designed to test their sense of touch and their ability to retain information about certain objects they have felt.

3. Next the group leader gives each participant a blindfold, a pencil, and a piece of paper. The participants are then asked to blindfold themselves.

4. When the blindfolds are in place, the trainer leads the participants, one at a time, to a table of objects. When all of the group members are at the table, the trainer removes the cloth and asks the participants, without talking, to feel the objects and try to imprint upon their minds the identity of each object.

5. After several minutes in which the participants move around the table and touch the objects, the trainer asks the group members to take one step back from the table. The group leader then places the tablecloth over the objects.

6. Next the group members remove their blindfolds

and, again without talking, return to their seats and list the objects they think they have felt.

7. When all of the participants have completed their lists, the trainer again uncovers the table and asks several group members to read their lists of items to the entire group.

8. The exercise may be processed through a discussion that focuses on the sense of touch and on any tricks the participants used to remember the items.

Variations

■ Following step #5 in the Trainer Administration section, the group leader may ask the participants to pair off and to discuss the exercise with their partners.

■ The trainer may ask all of the participants to turn their chairs away from the covered table. Then the trainer may solicit one volunteer to be blindfolded. The group leader uncovers the objects and leads the volunteer to the table. The volunteer then feels each object, and, without naming what he or she thinks the item is, describes how the object feels. For example: The volunteer may say, "The object is squishy, seems to be made of plastic, is bumpy, and seems to be about three inches wide and five inches long. Oh, it is damp." (The object is a kitchen sponge.) Based on the description and without talking, the group members write down what they think the item is. When the volunteer has felt and described all of the objects, the trainer covers the table. The volunteer removes his or her blindfold, the other group members turn their chairs around, and the group members then discuss their guesses. Finally, the trainer uncovers the table and names the objects in the order in which the volunteer described them.

Trainer's Notes

_____

_____

_____

_____

_____

_____

_____

Three-Legged Race

Activity
Summary This exercise is a game in which the participants, working in pairs, compete in a three-legged relay race. This icebreaker is effective at any time during the learning program.

**Training
Application**

Time Reference: Approximately 10 to 15 minutes.

Group Size: Best suited for a group of 16 or more participants.

Space Required: An unobstructed area without tables or chairs.

Materials Needed: Two strips of cloth that are three feet in length.

**Trainer
Administration**

1. The trainer begins by explaining that the group will be taking part in an old family-picnic favorite, the three-legged relay race.
2. The participants are to divide into two teams, with an equal number of group members on each team. If the group contains an uneven number, one participant may serve as a referee.
3. The members of each team are then instructed to form pairs.
4. The trainer asks the pairs on each team to line up behind an imaginary starting line. The group leader then places two chairs approximately 30 feet in front of the teams and approximately six feet apart.
5. The group leader then gives the first pair on each team a strip of cloth to wrap and then tie around their inside ankles.
6. The trainer explains that, when he or she says "Go," each pair is to race out around its team's chair and then back to the starting line. The partners then untie and unwrap the piece of cloth, pass it to the next pair, and go to the end of their team's line. The next partners then tie their legs together and move over the course, and so forth for all of the pairs on each team.
7. After explaining the game and giving the teams time to prepare their first pairs, the trainer says "Ready, set . . . go!" and the race begins.

8. The race continues until all of the team members have run the course. The winner is the team to finish first.

Variations
- The group leader may ask the participants to compete in a four-legged race, with three people tied together at the ankles.
- If the room is large enough, the trainer can ask the participants to pair off. Each pair is given a strip of cloth with which to join their inside ankles. All of the pairs then line up on an imaginary starting line. At a signal from the trainer, all of the pairs run out and then around one chair place 30 feet in front of the line. The winner is the pair to return to the starting line first.

Trainer's Notes

_____

_____

_____

_____

_____

_____

_____

_____

You Don't Say

This exercise challenges the participants, using clues that they are given, to identify the names of famous persons. This icebreaker in effective at any time during the learning program.

Time Reference: Approximately 15 to 20 minutes.

Group Size: Best suited for a group of 12 or more participants.

Space Required: A room that has the potential for flexible seating.

Materials Needed: Four chairs and trainer-prepared slips of paper with the names of famous persons written on them (two slips of paper for each famous name); for the trainer, the Sample Game Sheet (see the last page of this exercise).

1. The trainer asks the participants to divide into two groups, or teams, and to sit with their teammates.
2. The group leader then tells the teams that they will be challenging each other in a game that involves skill and intuition.
3. Next the trainer places four chairs in the front of the room and asks two people from each team to come forward and sit in the chairs, with the members of the same team facing each other.
4. The group leader explains that one team member will be the clue sender, while the other team member will serve as the clue receiver.
5. The group leader then explains the rules of the game.
   a. The trainer will give both clue senders slips of paper naming the same famous person.
   b. A toss of a coin will determine which team plays first.
   c. One at a time, the clue senders will use opposites to present clues. For example: If the famous person is Florence Nightingale, the clue sender might say, "The opposite of day is _____." (The clue sender can only give one clue; after giving the clue, he or she is not to speak until the next turn.)
   d. The clue receiver has 15 seconds in which to make as many attempts as he or she can to

identify the clue. However, the clue receiver can make only one guess per turn as to the name. If his or her guess is incorrect, the other team has a turn at giving and receiving clues. (The trainer may wish to read the Sample Games Sheet to the participants.)

e. The team of the player who guesses the name wins one point.

f. The clues must not be proper names.

g. The clues must be presented in sentence form.

h. The clues must not contain the name of the famous person.

i. The clue receiver must identify the clue correctly before he or she is allowed to guess the name of the famous person.

j. The clue sender may use gestures to help the receiver.

k. The clue receiver has only 15 seconds in which to identify the clue and to guess the identity of the famous person.

l. Observing team members may yell, shout, applaud, etc., but they cannot directly help their teammate in guessing the name.

6. After giving the instructions, the trainer tosses a coin and the winning team plays first. When one of the teams has been awarded a point, two new players from each team sit in the chairs and attempt to identify another famous person.

7. The game ends when one team has accumulated five points or when all of the participants have had an opportunity to play the game.

Variations

■ The trainer may conduct the activity as a group exercise. The participants form a circular seating arrangement. One volunteer comes forward to sit in the center of the circle and to serve as clue sender to the rest of the group. The volunteer may give one clue every 15 seconds. The first participant to guess correctly takes the volunteer's place, and a new famous name is given.

■ The group leader can use work- or study area-related phrases instead of famous names. For example: "Management by objectives," "Effective supervision pays off," "Reinforce good work," etc.

Trainer's Notes

_____

_____

_____

_____

_____

_____

_____

_____

_____

SAMPLE GAME SHEET

NAME: PAUL NEWMAN

FIRST TEAM
Sender: "The opposite of old is _____."
Receiver: "New. Wayne Newton." (wrong guess)

SECOND TEAM
Sender: "The opposite sex of a girl is a _____."
Receiver: "Boy." (The sender shakes his or her head.)
Receiver: "Man. (The sender nods his or her head.)
           Lorraine Newman." (wrong guess)

FIRST TEAM
Sender: "The opposite of short is _____."
Receiver: "Tall. Tall. . .man. . .new. . . .
           Tall. . .new. . .man. Paul Newman!"

GETTING
ACQUAINTED

Getting Acquainted

Whether or not a learning program emphasizes personal interaction among the participants, the use of getting-acquainted activities can provide a unique structure for lowering the barriers of group members. The ice-breakers in this division serve two primary functions: they establish non-threatening introductory contacts, and they increase the participants' familiarity with one another. These two functions can be key elements in the ultimate success or failure of many educational programs.

The initial meeting between participants often leads to the formation of impressions that will persist throughout the group's lifespan. Although first impressions are usually based upon incomplete or inaccurate information, they are used as reference points during later interactions. Getting-acquainted icebreakers will not necessarily eliminate invalid judgments or assessments, but they will offer group members the opportunity to experience one another in a balanced manner. This, in turn, will often lead to feelings of increased responsiveness and receptiveness. Obviously, the more comfortable the participants feel with one another, the greater becomes the likelihood for constructing a learning environment that welcomes new ideas and stimulates growth.

The second function, increased familiarity between participants, can be a vital aid for programs that desire to achieve a degree of group cohesiveness without focusing on intense personal exploration. In contrast to structuring mere introductions, several of the getting-acquainted activities are designed specifically to broaden the group members' exposure to one another during the ongoing stages of the group's development. These icebreakers increase the participants' familiarity with one another, without ``getting too personal.''

Regardless of the specific area of study, getting-acquainted icebreakers can bolster the learning process by increasing the group members' comfort level. In addition, the activities can be easily adapted to meet the specific needs of both the participants and the training program.

All Tied Up

Activity Summary

This exercise asks the participants to introduce themselves as they tie each other together. This activity is generally more effective when used in the early stage of the group's formation.

Training Application

Time Reference: Approximately 10 to 15 minutes.
Group Size: Unlimited, but best suited for a group of 20 or fewer participants.
Space Required: An unobstructed area without tables or chairs.
Materials Needed: A large ball of string.

Trainer Administration

1. After asking the group members to stand, the trainer explains that the participants will be introducing themselves as they tie each other's wrists.
2. The trainer then, at random, selects one participant and ties the end of a ball of string around his or her wrist. The trainer says, "My name is _____."
3. The trainer then instructs the participant to take the ball of string, walk to another person (preferably not the person right next to him or her), wind the cord loosely around that person's wrist, and say "My name is_____."
4. Keeping the string loosely wound around his or her wrist, that person is to take the ball of string to yet another participant, wind the cord loosely around the participant's wrist, and say "My name is _____."
5. As the exercise continues, the trainer may need to help the participant who has been tied and who must tie another group member. (The pattern of string in the room may ultimately resemble a piece of string art done by a toddler!)
6. The exercise concludes when all of the group members have been tied and introduced.

Variations

■ The trainer may request that the participant being tied respond to the introduction he or she receives by saying, "And my name is _____."

■ The trainer may request that as the group members unwind after step #5 in the Trainer Administration section, each participant repeat the name of the person who originally tied his or her wrist.
■ For athletic groups the trainer may allow the group members to tie wrists and ankles while introductions are made. Care must be taken so that the participants do not accidentally fall or trip.

Trainer's Notes

_____

_____

_____

_____

_____

_____

_____

Chair Mates

Activity Summary

This exercise is a guessing game in which the participants try to remember, or to use their intuition to guess, the names of other participants. This activity is generally more effective when used in the early stage of the group's formation.

Training Application

Time Reference: Approximately 15 to 20 minutes.

Group Size: Best suited for a group of 20 or more participants.

Space Required: A room that has the potential for flexible seating. The area must be large enough to permit the unrestricted movement of the learners.

Materials Needed: For the trainer, a roster of the participants' names.

Trainer Administration

1. The trainer begins the exercise by asking the group members, one at a time, to state their names.
2. Next the group members are to form a circular seating arrangement.
3. When the participants are seated, the group leader divides them into groups by asking them to count off by two: one—two—one—two, etc.
4. The trainer then tells the participants that the groups, to be referred to as group 1 and group 2, will be playing a guessing game in which they will be challenged to remember their fellow participants' names.
5. Next the group leader explains the rules of the game.
   a. The members of group 1 will be asked to leave the room.
   b. Each member of group 2 will then stand behind his or her chair.
   c. At a signal from the trainer, group 1 will send one of its members into the room. The trainer will tell him or her the full name of one of the participants in group 2.
   d. The member of group 1 must then sit in the chair in front of the participant he or she thinks has just been named. If the group member chooses the correct chair, he or she remains seated.

e. If the member from group 1 chooses incorrectly, the members of group 2 begin clapping and continue to clap until the person from group 1 finds the chair that belongs to the person who has been named.

f. Another person from group 1 enters the room, and the process continues until all of the members of group 2 are seated according to the names the trainer has called.

g. Then the entire exercise is repeated with the members of group 1 leaving the room and the members of group 2 standing behind their chairs.

6. When the rules have been explained, the trainer asks the members of group 1 to leave the room, and the game begins.

7. The game continues until both groups have had an opportunity to test their ability to remember their fellow participants' names.

Variations

■ Since the exercise becomes easier as more group members identify names and are seated in the proper chairs, the trainer may ask that once a member of the group outside the room has entered and identified a person, he or she not remain seated but instead move and sit in his or her own chair. Thus, each group member will have the same degree of difficulty in matching his or her assigned name to the correct person.

■ The trainer can use a point system in conducting the exercise. When the members of group 2 are all standing behind their chairs, the trainer calls all of the members of group 1 back into the room. The group leader then reads a name, and all of the members of group 1, without talking, scramble for that person's chair; more than one participant can choose the same chair. When everyone is seated, the person whose name has been called identifies himself or herself. The participant(s) occupying the person's chair receive(s) one point. The trainer then reads off another name, and the process continues until all of the names of the members of group 2 have been read. The members of group 2 leave the room, and the exercise is repeated.

Trainer's Notes

_____

_____

_____

_____

_____

_____

_____

_____

_____

Clap, Clap, Clap, Snap

Activity Summary

This exercise uses a rhythm game to help the participants learn one another's names. This activity is most effective when used in the early stage of the group's formation.

Training Application

Time Reference: Approximately 10 to 15 minutes.
Group Size: Best suited for a group of 10 to 20 participants.
Space Required: A room that has the potential for flexible seating.
Materials Needed: Black markers, masking tape, and, for each participant, a piece of paper.

Trainer Administration

1. The group leader asks the participants to form a circular seating arrangement.
2. When the participants are seated, the trainer gives each group member a piece of paper and then distributes markers and pieces of masking tape.
3. Explaining that this activity is designed to help the group members learn each other's names, the trainer instructs the participants to write their names on their pieces of paper in letters that are large enough to be read by the entire group. The participants are to tape their name tags to the right legs of their chairs. The group members are then given several minutes to look at and become familiar with one another's names.
4. Next the trainer tells the group members to stand and move one seat to the right. When the participants are in their new seats, the group leader randomly selects one chair to serve as the leader of the circle. The leader chair remains the same throughout the game.
5. The trainer then explains the rhythm portion of the game. The participants are to clap their hands three times and then snap their fingers one time: clap—clap—clap—snap. The trainer leads a brief practice of the rhythm, performing the clapping and snapping very slowly at first and then establishing the tempo at which the game is to be played.
6. The group leader tells the participants that on the snap the person in the leader chair is to call out someone's name. The person sitting in the chair

that has that name taped to it must say "Here I am!" before the third clap and on the next snap call out another name. The group member responsible for the new name must again respond before the third clap and on the next snap call out yet another name. At this point the trainer may wish to conduct a brief practice game.

7. The trainer then directs the group member in the leader chair to begin the game. The game continues until someone fails to respond before the third clap or fails to call out a new name on the next snap. The person in error must leave the circle, while everyone else moves one chair to the right. Now each participant has a new name (the name taped to the chair in which he or she is sitting) to be responsible for on the snap.

8. The game, which the trainer may complicate by quickly speeding up the tempo of the clap-snap sequence, continues for five minutes or until only three players remain.

Variation

■ The trainer may tell the participants to change seats at any point in the game. All of the group members continue the clap-snap rhythm but move one seat to the left or right (depending on the trainer's instructions) and become responsible for a new name.

Trainer's Notes

Color, Car, Character

Activity Summary

This exercise asks the participants to introduce themselves by naming colors, cars, and fictional characters that represent aspects of their own personalities. This activity is generally more effective when used in the early stage of the group's formation.

Training Application

Time Reference: Approximately 15 to 20 minutes.

Group Size: Best suited for a group of 10 to 20 participants.

Space Required: A room that is large enough to accommodate the comfortable seating of the participants.

Materials Needed: For each participant, a pencil and a piece of paper.

Trainer Administration

1. While distributing paper and pencils to all of the participants, the trainer explains that the group members will be taking part in an activity that is designed to help them become acquainted with one another.

2. The group leader then asks that each participant write his or her name on the piece of paper. Under his or her name each participant is to write a color which he or she feels fits his or her personality. Beneath the color the participant is to write the name of a car that he or she thinks is appropriate to his or her self-image. Finally, under the name of the car, the participant is to write the name of a fictional character with whom he or she identifies.

3. Then, one at a time, the group members introduce themselves by stating their names, colors, cars, and fictional characters. In the introduction, each participant is to provide a brief rationale for each of his or her three choices. For example: "I see myself as a Volkswagen because I am practical and am concerned about economic factors."

4. The exercise continues until all of the participants have introduced themselves by color, car, and character.

Variations

■ If the group contains more than 20 participants, the trainer may ask the group members to give only one description of themselves, such as their relation to a particular color, car, or character.

■ The group leader may request that the participants relate themselves to various kinds of insects, flowers, foods, games, film stars, political figures, or any combination of these.

■ The trainer may ask that each participant give his or her name and then act out one or all of the chosen descriptions while the other group members attempt to guess the particular color, car, or fictional character he or she has selected.

Trainer's Notes

_____

_____

_____

_____

_____

_____

_____

Completed Thought

Activity Summary

This exercise helps the participants get acquainted with others by sharing their thoughts about certain issues. This structured experience is most appropriate for educational programs or sessions that emphasize personal interaction among group members. This icebreaker is effective at any time during the learning program.

Training Application

Time Reference: Approximately 25 to 30 minutes.

Group Size: Unlimited, but best suited for a group of 10 to 20 participants.

Space Required: A room that is large enough to permit the unrestricted movement of the learners.

Materials Needed: For each participant, a pencil and a piece of paper; for the trainer, a copy of the Statements to be Completed List (see the last page of this exercise).

Trainer Administration

1. The group leader begins by stating that this learning experience is designed to explore the participants' thought processes.

2. After giving each participant a pencil and a piece of paper, the trainer explains that the group members will be listening to a series of incomplete statements. The participants will be writing down the statement and then, using their own words, completing the thought. For example: "If I could be anyone, I would be _____."

3. The group leader then reads the first incomplete sentence to the participants (see the Statements to be Completed Sheet). After giving the group members one minute to copy down and then complete the thought, the trainer proceeds to the second statement, continuing the aforementioned process until the participants have completed all 10 statements.

4. When the participants have finished, the trainer rereads the statements one at a time and asks each group member to share his or her responses with the group. At any interval, the group members may discuss or question the rationale for a participant's response.

5. The trainer may conclude the activity by discussing the similarities and differences among the group members' responses.

Variations   ■ The trainer may formulate a list of statements that corresponds to the training agenda. For example: A workshop on creativity may use statements such as "I am most creative when _____," "When I look at a picture, I look for _____," etc.

■ If the group contains more than 20 participants, the trainer may divide the participants into work groups of five or six members each. Following the completion of step #3 in the Trainer Administration section, the members of the work group share their responses with one another.

■ The trainer may ask the participants to sign their names to their statements and to post them around the room for everyone to see.

Trainer's Notes

_____

_____

_____

_____

_____

_____

_____

_____

STATEMENTS TO BE COMPLETED LIST

1. Today I wish I were _____ .

2. The main reason I am here is _____ .

3. When I think of my work, I _____ .

4. People who smoke are_____ .

5. My boss and I are _____ .

6. I choose friends who are_____ .

7. I think my best quality is my_____ .

8. Training sessions like this are usually _____ .

9. Today I am planning\to learn_____ .

10. A pet peeve of mine is _____ .

Crisscross Handshake

This exercise has the participants greet one another by shaking hands according to a specific pattern. This activity is generally more effective when used in the early stage of the group's formation.

**Training
Application**
Time Reference: Approximately 5 to 10 minutes.
Group Size: Unlimited, but best suited for a group of 10 or more participants.
Space Required: An unobstructed area without tables or chairs. The room must be large enough to permit the unrestricted movement of the learners.
Materials Needed: None

**Trainer
Administration**
1. The trainer asks the group members to stand and, if necessary, clear the room of any obstacles. The participants are to form two lines, with an equal number of group members in each line. The participants in one line should face the participants in the other line; the lines should be at least three feet apart.
2. The group leader explains that in this quick-moving exercise the group members will be introducing themselves to and shaking hands with each other according to a specific format and pattern.
3. The persons at the heads of the two lines are to be the leaders. Simultaneously both leaders walk across to the line opposite that in which each was standing. The leader of the first line introduces himself or herself to and shakes hands with the person who was standing next to the leader of the second line, while the leader of the second line introduces himself or herself to the person who was standing next to the leader of the first line.
4. In performing an introduction, the leader must state his or her name; the person receiving the leader's greeting must respond with his or her own name. Example: The leader shakes hands and says, "My name is Robyn Neal,"; the person responds, "And I am Chris Raymond."
5. After crossing back to his or her original line, each leader shakes hands and performs introductions with the person next to the one the other leader has already greeted. The leaders continue this

pattern, crisscrossing back and forth, each leader greeting every other person in each line (see Diagram of Handshake below).

6. When the leaders have gone through both lines, they become the last persons in each line. Then the next persons at the head of the lines become the leaders, repeating the process of introducing themselves, shaking hands, and receiving the return greetings of the persons whose hands they shake.

7. The exercise continues until the original leaders are again at the beginning of each line.

Diagram of Handshake

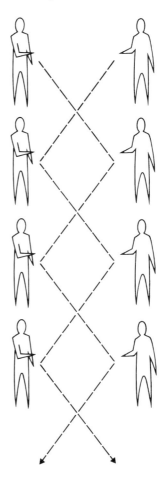

■ The group leader can add a humorous note to the exercise by urging the line leaders to move more quickly through the introductions.

■ When a set of leaders has finished going through the lines, the trainer can ask each leader to repeat the names of the people he or she has met.

■ The group leader can conduct the exercise in a simpler manner by having the participants form one line. The line leader introduces himself or herself to each person down the line and, in turn, receives the names of the persons he or she meets. The next participant in line follows immediately after the line leader, and is followed by the third participant, and so on until the initial line leader is again at the head of the line.

Trainer's Notes

_____

_____

_____

_____

_____

_____

_____

_____

Duo Interviews

**Activity
Summary** This exercise asks the participants, working in pairs, to prepare and then present introductions of each other to the entire group. This activity is generally more effective when used in the early stage of the group's formation.

**Training
Application** *Time Reference:* Approximately 15 to 20 minutes.
Group Size: Unlimited, but best suited for a group of 10 to 20 participants.
Space Required: A room that has the potential for flexible seating. Several small meeting rooms or areas that provide private or semiprivate interaction are also needed.
Materials Needed: None.

**Trainer
Administration**
1. The trainer begins the exercise by explaining that this getting-acquainted activity asks the participants to introduce one another to the group.
2. Next the group leader asks the participants to pair off, preferably with persons they do not know or do not know well. (If the group members are hesitant, the trainer may wish to assign partners. Should it be necessary, one group may contain three members.)
3. Each pair is to find a place in which the partners can work with some degree of privacy. They are then to spend five minutes interviewing each other, learning each other's names and sharing information about backgrounds, interests, values, goals, etc.
4. The group leader may wish to call out the time when one minute remains so that both partners have an opportunity to share information about themselves.
5. When the allotted time has elapsed, the trainer calls the group together.
6. When the group has assembled, the trainer explains that the partners are to introduce each other to the group. The participant performing the introduction is to stand behind his or her partner's chair and to speak as if he or she were that person. For example: "My name is Tom. I have a wife and two boys. I was born and reared in California, but

I moved to Illinois two years ago because of the job I now hold as a sales representative. I enjoy backpacking and jogging."

7. The group leader solicits a pair to volunteer to begin the introductions. The exercise continues until all of the group members have been introduced.

Variations ■ If the members of a group appear to be uninhibited, the group leader can ask the partners to perform the introductions by acting out each other's key characteristics or personal traits.

■ The trainer can encourage the group members to ask questions about the person who is being introduced. The partner must answer the questions to the best of his or her ability. Then the person being introduced responds as to the accuracy of his or her partner's statements.

Trainer's Notes

Fantasy Island

Activity Summary

This exercise encourages the participants to become better acquainted as they create fantasized selves that they then introduce to the group. This activity is generally more effective when used in the early stage of the group's formation.

Training Application

Time Reference: Approximately 15 to 20 minutes.

Group Size: Best suited for a group of 10 to 20 participants. If the group contains more than 20 participants, subgroups should be formed.

Space Required: A room that is large enough to accommodate the comfortable seating of the participants.

Materials Needed: For each participant, a pencil and a piece of paper; for the trainer, a copy of the Fantasy Sheet (see the last page of this exercise).

Trainer Administration

1. The trainer explains that in this exercise the participants will be taking a journey into the world of fantasy.

2. The participants are instructed to sit comfortably, close their eyes, and think of or create a person they would like to be. They may be guided to consider the following questions: If they had total freedom of choice, who would they like to be? What are the characteristics of this person's life? What wonderful qualities does this person possess? At what time in history does/did/will this person live? The trainer tells the group members that they are to attempt to become their fantasy persons.

3. While the group members are constructing their fantasies, the trainer gives each participant a pencil and a piece of paper. The trainer then tells the participants to open their eyes and within five minutes to write a brief (one or two paragraphs) autobiography of their fantasy selves. The trainer may wish to illustrate the exercise by reading the Fantasy Sheet to the group (see the last page of this exercise).

4. When the allotted time has elapsed, the trainer solicits a volunteer to read his or her autobiography to the other inhabitants of Fantasy Island.

Then the volunteer is to reveal his or her true identity and to explain briefly his or her choice of that particular fantasy.

5. This exercise continues until all of the participants have read and discussed their fantasies.

Variations
■ The trainer may request that as they read, the participants adopt the voice inflections and mannerisms of their fantasy beings.

■ The group leader may collect the autobiographies and then read each one out loud, while the group members try to decide which of their fellow participants has chosen a particular fantasy.

■ If the group members appear to be uninhibited, the trainer may direct them to construct a fantasy around being an animal. Each participant then acts as his or her chosen animal, while the group members attempt to guess its identity.

Trainer's Notes

FANTASY SHEET

My name is Brandon O'Shea. I was born in poverty in the northern part of Ireland, but I created the shamrock symbol which has made me rich and famous. I now travel around the country on my yacht or tour the world in my private jet; I create an international stir wherever I land. I love to give away new cars to strangers who smile at me. My two biggest problems in life are fighting off beautiful women and not being able to give my money away as fast as I would like.

Finders

Activity Summary This exercise helps the participants become better acquainted as they match their perceptions or impressions of their fellow participants to a list of descriptive statements. This activity is generally more effective when used in the early stage of the group's formation.

Training Application

Time Reference: Approximately 20 to 25 minutes.

Group Size: Best suited for a group of 10 to 20 participants.

Space Required: A room that is large enough to permit the unrestricted movement of the learners.

Materials Needed: For each participant, a pencil and a copy of the Finder's Sheet (see the last page of this exercise).

Trainer Administration

1. The trainer begins by explaining that the group members will be taking part in an exercise that is designed to help them become better acquainted with one another.

2. Next the group leader gives each participant a pencil and a copy of the Finder's Sheet.

3. The participants are then instructed to stand up, mill around the room, and locate, based upon their perceptions or impressions, a person that fits each of the descriptions given in the Finder's Sheet.

4. At each "finding," the participant introduces himself or herself to that person and explains what description the person fits. For example: "You appear to fit item #1 on the Finder's Sheet in that you seem to be someone who enjoys children; you have soft, gentle eyes. My name is Carolyn Brown. What is your name? . . . Thank you." The participant writes that person's name next to the appropriate description and then moves on to seek another "finding."

5. When the participants have completed their Finder's Sheets, they are to introduce themselves to all of the other participants they have not as yet met.

Variations

■ The group leader may formulate a Finder's Sheet that focuses on work-related characteristics. For example: Find someone who appears to be a flexible supervisor; find someone who looks as if he or she works well with others; find someone who seems to be efficient.

■ If the group contains fewer than 15 members, the trainer may ask each participant to explain to the entire group his or her choice for each category on the Finder's Sheet.

**Trainer's
Notes**

_____

_____

_____

_____

_____

_____

_____

_____

FINDER'S SHEET

1. Find someone who looks as if he or she enjoys children.

   Name: _____

2. Find someone who looks as if he or she likes to play sports.

   Name: _____

3. Find someone who looks as if he or she loves animals.

   Name: _____

4. Find someone who looks as if he or she is ambitious.

   Name: _____

5. Find someone who looks as if he or she appreciates classical music.

   Name: _____

6. Find someone who looks as if he or she likes exciting activities.

   Name: _____

7. Find someone who looks as if he or she is an interesting conversationalist.

   Name: _____

8. Find someone who looks as if he or she enjoys spicy food.

   Name: _____

9. Find someone who looks sophisticated.

   Name: _____

10. Find someone who looks intelligent.

    Name: _____

Follow the Leader

Activity
Summary This exercise helps the participants become acquainted as they repeat one another's names and favorite activities. This activity is most effective when used in the early stage of the group's formation.

Training
Application *Time Reference:* Approximately 10 to 15 minutes.
Group Size: Best suited for a group of 10 to 20 participants.
Space Required: A room that has the potential for flexible seating.
Materials Needed: None.

Trainer
Administration 1. The group leader asks the participants to form a circular seating arrangement.
2. When the participants are seated, the trainer explains that since this exercise is designed to help them become better acquainted with one another, the group members are first to think of something they enjoy doing.
3. The group leader then solicits a volunteer to begin the activity. The volunteer is to say his or her first name and then mention some activity or pastime he or she enjoys. The person to the volunteer's right is to repeat what the volunteer has said and then add his or her name and favorite activity. The next person repeats what the others have said and adds his or her personal information. For example: "His name is David, and he likes to eat; her name is Sarah, and she likes to read; and my name is Ann, and I like to sail."
4. Group members may, at any time, help a person who has some difficulty remembering a particular name or activity.
5. The exercise continues around the circle until the last person (or the trainer) has repeated all of the names and activities and added his or her name and personal information.

Variations ■ If the group contains more than 25 participants, the trainer may ask the group members to give and repeat names only.
■ During the middle of the exercise, the group leader may ask various participants to exchange

seats to ensure that the group members are truly becoming acquainted and not just memorizing names and/or information in a particular sequence.

Trainer's Notes

Groupings

Activity Summary

This exercise uses a grouping process to help the participants become acquainted with one another. This activity is generally more effective when used in the early stage of the group's formation.

Training Application

Time Reference: Approximately 35 to 40 minutes.

Group Size: Best suited for a group of 16 to 32 participants.

Space Required: A room that is large enough to permit the unrestricted movement of the learners. Several small meeting rooms or areas that provide private or semiprivate interaction are also needed.

Materials Needed: None.

Trainer Administration

1. The trainer tells the group members that they will be participating in an exercise that will help them become better acquainted with one another.

2. First the participants are instructed to line up according to height. Next the group leader divides them into pairs, matching the tallest group member with the shortest participant, the next tallest with the next shortest, and so on until all of the participants have partners. If necessary, one group can contain three members.

3. The trainer then tells the pairs to locate private or semi-private areas in which they can spend five minutes introducing themselves and then sharing their recent professional or personal accomplishments.

4. When they have finished their discussion, each pair is to return to the group meeting area and, remaining together, to locate another pair. The pairs introduce themselves and discuss personal or professional goals.

5. After 10 minutes the trainer asks each foursome to select and then join another foursome. For 15 minutes the participants introduce themselves and share what they feel are their personal or professional strengths.

6. The trainer calls all of the group members together and initiates a discussion in which the participants talk about their reactions to the activity and the impact of their first impressions.

Variations ■ The trainer can continue the exercise by joining the subgroups until all of the participants are again in one large group.

■ The trainer may instruct the original pairs to be responsible for introducing each other to the members of each new group they join.

■ For smaller groups the trainer can eliminate step #5 in the Trainer Administration section.

Trainer's Notes

_____

_____

_____

_____

_____

_____

_____

_____

Human Sandwich

Activity Summary

This exercise asks the participants to make sandwich boards, writing on one side what they already know about themselves and on the other side what they would like to know about themselves. This structured exercise is most appropriate for educational programs or sessions that emphasize personal interaction among group members. This icebreaker is effective at any time during the learning program.

Training Application

Time Reference: Approximately 15 to 20 minutes.

Group Size: Unlimited, but best suited for a group of 10 to 20 participants.

Space Required: A room that contains adequate writing space for all of the participants. The area must be large enough to permit the unrestricted movement of the learners.

Materials Needed: For each participant, two sheets of newsprint, a colored marker, and at least two straight pins or strips of masking tape.

Trainer Administration

1. After giving each participant two sheets of newsprint, a colored marker, and several straight pins or strips of masking tape, the trainer explains that the group members will be sharing with others their knowledge about themselves.

2. At the top of one sheet of newsprint, each participant is to write "What I Know about Myself" and at the top of the other sheet, "What I Want to Know about Myself."

3. The group members are then given 10 minutes in which to write words, phrases, and/or sentences that capture what they know and wish to know about themselves.

4. When the allotted time has elapsed, each participant is to pin or tape the "What I Know about Myself" sheet on his or her front and the "What I Want to Know about Myself" sheet on his or her back.

5. The trainer then instructs the group members to mill about the room and to look at each other's sandwich boards. They may stop and discuss each other's boards at any time.

Variations   ■ The group leader may choose headings that relate specifically to the workshop agenda. For example: "The Things That Cause Strees in My Life" and "The Things That Relax Me" are appropriate headings for a workshop on stress management.

■ The trainer may choose headings that are less threatening than those given in step #2 of the Trainer Administration section. For example: "Things I Like" and "Things I Don't Like" or "My Favorite Things to Do" and "My Least Favorite Things to Do."

■ After the completion of step #5 in the Trainer Administration section, the group leader may ask the participants to pair off, choosing partners they feel are similar to themselves. The partners then are given additional time in which to learn more about each other.

Trainer's Notes

_____

_____

_____

_____

_____

_____

_____

_____

Identification

Activity Summary This exercise asks the participants to share some important personal information that is revealed by what they carry in their purses/wallets/billfolds. This activity is generally more effective when used in the early stage of the group's formation.

Training Application

Time Reference: Approximately 10 minutes.

Group Size: Best suited for a group of 10 to 20 participants.

Space Required: A room that is large enough to accommodate the comfortable seating of the participants.

Materials Needed: For each participant, his or her own purse/wallet/billfold.

Trainer Administration

1. The trainer begins the activity by explaining that the group members will be introducing themselves in an unusual manner.
2. The group leader then instructs the participants to look in their purses/wallets/billfolds and to find something that is representative or symbolic of their personal or professional characteristics or skills. For example: a picture, a club membership card, a dollar bill, etc.
3. After several minutes the trainer asks that each participant share his or her name and identify the item he or she has chosen. Then the group member is to explain briefly why that object is representative or symbolic of his or her skills or traits.
4. The exercise continues until all of the participants have introduced themselves and shared their chosen objects with the entire group.

Variations

■ The trainer may request that the participants form pairs. (If necessary, one group may contain three members.) After the partners have individually chosen their objects, they briefly discuss the significance of each item. Then the partners are responsible for introducing one another and then explaining the significance of each other's objects to the entire group. (This variation requires at least 20 minutes.)

■ The group leader may ask the participants first to introduce themselves by name only. Then each group member passes his or her object around, while the other participants attempt to guess, based on first impressions, what that object symbolizes or represents to the group member. The individual may respond to the other group members' interpretations of his or her object.

Trainer's Notes

_____

_____

_____

_____

_____

_____

_____

Know Your States

Activity Summary
This exercise, which is designed to move individuals into groups, asks the participants to form pairs based on the names of states and their capitals and then to join other pairs to form regions. This activity is generally more effective when used in the early stage of the group's formation.

Training Application

Time Reference: Approximately 15 to 20 minutes.

Group Size: Best suited for a group of 12 or more participants.

Space Required: A room that has the potential for flexible seating. The area must be large enough to permit the unrestricted movement of the learners.

Materials Needed: For each participant, a trainer-prepared slip of paper with the name of either a state or its capital written on it; for the trainer, a map of the United States upon which the states have been divided into regions: Northeast, Middle Atlantic, Southeast, Midwest, Southwest, and Far West.

Trainer Administration

1. The group leader explains that in this exercise the participants will first pair off and then form larger work groups.

2. After giving each group member a slip of paper with either the name of a state or its capital written on it, the trainer directs the participants to locate the person who has the state or capital name that corresponds to the name he or she holds.

3. After matching their state and capital names, the partners briefly introduce themselves to each other.

4. The capital-state name pairs are then instructed to join together with other pairs to form one of the six basic regions in the United States: Northeast, Middle Atlantic, Southeast, Midwest, Southwest, and Far West. The partners may refer to the trainer's map if they are uncertain about the region to which their state belongs. (For smaller groups, fewer regions will be used.)

5. The trainer then asks the group members in each region to introduce themselves to one another.

6. The regional groups that are formed can then serve as the work groups for another activity.

Variations

■ When the participants have formed regions, the trainer can ask them to discuss a specific topic from the study area. For example: In a stress management workshop, the group members can discuss those factors that contribute to undue stress in the professional setting.

■ The group leader can ask the members of all of the regions to join together, thus reassembling the large group. The members of each region then briefly introduce themselves to members of other regions.

Trainer's Notes

_____

_____

_____

_____

_____

_____

_____

_____

Life Events

Activity Summary

This exercise uses the participants' drawings of themselves to help them become better acquainted with one another. This structured experience is most appropriate for educational programs or sessions that emphasize personal interaction among group members. This icebreakerr is effective at any time during the learning program.

Training Application

Time Reference: Approximately 20 to 25 minutes.

Group Size: Unlimited, but best suited for a group of 10 to 20 participants.

Space Required: A room that contains adequate writing space for all of the participants. The area must be large enough to permit the unrestricted movement of the learners.

Materials Needed: For each participant, a large sheet of newsprint and three crayons or colored markers.

Trainer Administration

1. The trainer begins by explaining that the group members will be taking part in an exercise that is designed to help them become better acquainted with their fellow participants.

2. After instructing the group members to seat themselves at tables, the trainer gives each participant a sheet of newsprint and three crayons or colored markers.

3. Holding up a sheet of newsprint, the trainer demonstrates how the participants are to fold the paper in half and then in half again so that the paper is divided into four boxes. Next the participants fold their papers, unfold them, and outline the fold marks in crayon or marker.

4. The trainer then asks each participant to write the following headings at the top of the boxes: Childhood (top left box), Teenage Years (top right box), Adult Life (bottom left box), and Future (bottom right box) (see Diagram of Life Events Boxes).

5. The group leader explains that in each of the Childhood, Teenage Years, and Adult Life boxes, the participants are each to draw a simple picture that outlines an event or action that was extremely important to that particular stage of their life. In

the Future box, they are each to draw a picture of an event or action that they *hope* will change or add to their life.

6. The group members then are given 15 minutes in which to complete their drawings.

7. When the allotted time has elapsed, the trainer asks the participants to divide into groups of four or five and to share their life events with one another.

Diagram of Life Events Boxes

Childhood	Teenage Years
Adult Life	Future

Variations

■ The trainer may use different headings in the four boxes. For example: My Life Ten Years Ago, My Life Five Years Ago, My Life Now, and My Life in the Future.

■ The group leader may request that the participants write about, instead of draw, an event for each box.

■ If the group contains fewer than 12 participants the trainer may request that the group member share their life events with the entire group.

■ Using the headings presented in step #4 of the Trainer Administration section, the group leader may direct the participants to depict in the first three boxes the most exciting or amusing event that occurred during each time period. The fourth box, Future, is to contain their secret or fantasy ambition.

Trainer's Notes

_____

_____

_____

_____

_____

_____

_____

_____

_____

Person Poem

Activity Summary

This exercise helps the participants become acquainted as they share poems they have written about themselves. This activity is generally more effective when used in the early stage of the group's formation.

Training Application

Time Reference: Approximately 15 to 20 minutes.

Group Size: Unlimited, but best suited for a group of 10 to 20 participants.

Space Required: A room that contains adequate writing space for all of the group members. The area must be large enough to accommodate the comfortable seating of the participants.

Materials Needed: For each participant, a pencil and a piece of paper.

Trainer Administration

1. The trainer informs the group members that in this exercise they will be writing short poems about themselves and then sharing these poems with the entire group.

2. The group leader explains that each poem is to be at least four lines long and must include the participant's name and some information about his or her personality, interests, occupation, life style, etc. For example: "My hobby is golf/And my name is Ken Stone/I work in a bank/ and I live all alone."

3. The trainer then gives each participant a pencil and a piece of paper and tells the group members that they have three minutes in which to write their poems.

4. When the allotted time has elapsed, the trainer solicits a volunteer to read his or her poem out loud to the group. The activity continues until all of the participants have shared their poems.

Variations

■ The trainer may request that each poem contain a reason for the participant's being in the training program or session.

■ The group leader may ask the participants to pair off and spend several minutes becoming acquainted. Next the partners write poems about each other and then share their creations with the entire group.

■ If the group contains fewer than 10 members, the trainer may ask each participant to write a poem that is between 8 and 12 lines in length and that contains more information about his or her activities, interests, goals, talents, shortcomings, etc.

■ The group leader may instruct the participants to write short poems describing themselves and their interests but not giving their names. The trainer collects the poems and then reads each one out loud, while the group members attempt to guess the identity of the poet.

Trainer's Notes

_____

_____

_____

_____

_____

_____

_____

_____

Philosophy of Work

Activity
Summary This exercise asks the participants to write short sentences about their philosophies of work and to respond nonverbally to other group members' statements of philosophy. This activity is generally more effective when used in the early stage of the group's formation.

Training Application

Time Reference: Approximately 15 to 20 minutes.

Group Size: Best suited for a group of 10 to 20 participants.

Space Required: An unobstructed area without tables or chairs. The room must be large enough to permit the unrestricted movement of the learners.

Materials Needed: For each participant, a pencil and a small piece of note paper.

Trainer Administration

1. While giving each participant a pencil and a piece of note paper, the trainer explains that the group members will be taking part in an exercise that is designed to help them become acquainted with one another.

2. Each person is then instructed to write one sentence, slogan, or phrase that describes his or her philosophy of work.

3. Next, without speaking, the participants are to stand and, holding their pencils and papers, to circulate among their fellow group members until they have each selected a partner. (If the group contains an uneven number, the trainer will need to take part in the exercise.)

4. Next the partners exchange papers and read one another's philosophies, responding nonverbally to what each of them has written. For example: They may smile broadly, nod agreement, raise their eyebrows in surprise, etc.

5. After this exchange, each person takes back his or her paper and immediately moves to a new partner. The new partners exchange papers and respond nonverbally to each other's statements. They then move to new partners and repeat the procedure.

6. The trainer allows approximately 10 minutes for the participants to move around the room and

nonverbally exchange information with other group members. The trainer may need to remind the group members that the exercise is a nonverbal one.

7. When the allotted time has elapsed, the trainer calls the participants together and asks them, one at a time, to share their names with the rest of the group. The exercise may then be processed through a discussion in which the group members share their feelings, thoughts, and impressions of each other as realized through what they have just experienced.

Variations ■ The trainer may request that, instead of their philosophy of work, the participants describe one of their goals or reveal one of their favorite fantasies.

■ The group leader may conduct the exercise verbally. The participants circulate and then form pairs. The partners share their philosophies and verbally react to each other's statements. The pairs then break up and move on to seek other partners with whom they can discuss their ideas about work.

Trainer's Notes

_____

_____

_____

_____

_____

_____

_____

Picassos

This exercise, which is designed to help the group members become better acquainted, asks the participants to do abstract drawings of one another. This directed experience is best implemented after the participants have had some opportunity to engage in feedback and disclosure during the learning program.

Training Application

Time Reference: Approximately 20 to 30 minutes.

Group Size: Best suited for a group of 10 to 20 participants.

Space Required: A room that has the potential for flexible seating.

Materials Needed: For each participant, a sheet of newsprint and several crayons.

Trainer Administration

1. The trainer asks the group members to form a circular seating arrangement.
2. When the group members are seated, the trainer explains that the participants will be creating works of art for a traveling show being sponsored by the Guggenheim Museum of New York City. The participants are going to draw abstract pictures of their fellow group members.
3. After giving each participant a sheet of newsprint and three or four crayons, the trainer asks that each group member study the person sitting to his or her right, paying close attention to the person's profile, manner of dress, and any behavioral traits that can be identified or inferred.
4. The trainer then explains that each participant is, at the top of his or her paper, to write the name of this neighbor. Within five minutes, the participant is to do an abstract drawing that represents what he or she feels is the person's personality. The group leader may wish to show the participants a sample abstract painting or drawing that will illustrate the type of drawing to be done or to mention the names of, or display prints of works by, familiar modern artists whose style might inspire the group members. For example: Picasso, Chagall, Klee, Miro, etc.

5. When the participants have finished their drawings, the trainer directs them to write at the bottom of the paper five adjectives that they feel describe the person they have drawn.
6. The exercise concludes after the participants, one at a time, have shared their drawings and observations with the entire group.

Variations
■ The trainer may ask the participants to pair off and then do drawings of each other.
■ The group leader may direct the participants to complete steps #1 through 5 in the Trainer Administration section but not write the subjects' names on the drawings. The group leader then collects the drawings and displays them one at a time while the group members attempt to guess the name of the person portrayed. When all of the pictures have been shown, the artist and model for each work identify themselves.

Trainer's Notes

_____

_____

_____

_____

_____

_____

_____

_____

Press Release

Activity Summary

This exercise helps the participants become acquainted as they work in pairs to create press releases for one another. This activity is generally more effective when used in the early stage of the group's formation.

Training Application

Time Reference: Approximately 25 to 30 minutes.

Group Size: Best suited for a group of 10 or more participants.

Space Required: A room that is large enough to accomodate the comfortable seating of the participants. Several small meeting rooms or areas that provide private or semiprivate interaction are also needed.

Materials Needed: For each participant, a black marker and a piece of paper.

Trainer Administration

1. The trainer explains that this get-acquainted exercise asks the group members to pair off and, working together, write press releases for each other.

2. The group leader tells the participants that the essential elements for each press release are name, occupation, and some information about why the participant is attending the workshop or program and what he or she hopes to gain from the experience.

3. The trainer then requests that the group members form pairs. (If the group contains an uneven number of participants, one group of three may be formed.) When the pairs have formed, the trainer explains that the partners will have seven minutes in which to interview each other and write both press releases.

4. The partners then disperse to locate areas in which each pair can work with some degree of privacy.

5. When the allotted time has elapsed, the trainer reassembles the large group. A volunteer is solicited to stand and read his or her partner's press release to the entire group.

6. The exercise continues until all of the participants have introduced themselves.

Variations
- The trainer may request that the press releases focus solely on such professional data as goals, unique talents or skills, special achievements, etc.
- The group leader may ask that the press releases contain information that relates to the agenda of the workshop or training program. For example: If the training is focused on supervisory skills, the press releases may contain information on present skills and skills the participants wish to acquire.
- The trainer may request that the group members work individually to prepare their own press releases.
- The group leader may direct the participants to divide into groups of four. The work group members then cooperatively write a press release for each group member.

Trainer's Notes

_____

_____

_____

_____

_____

_____

_____

_____

Salt Lips

Activity Summary

This exercise asks the participants to eat two saltine crackers and then immediately introduce themselves by stating their names and sharing one of their positive characteristics or skills. This structured experience is generally more effective when used in the early stage of the group's formation.

Training Application

Time Reference: Approximately 5 to 10 minutes.
Group Size: Unlimited.
Space Required: A room that has the potential for flexible seating.
Materials Needed: For each participant, two saltine crackers.

Trainer Administration

1. The trainer first asks the group members to form a circular seating arrangement.
2. When the participants are seated, the group leader explains that they will be introducing themselves to one another by stating their names and then giving one personal characteristic or skill that they are proud of.
3. While giving each group two saltine crackers, the trainer tells the participants that before introducing themselves, they must eat the crackers.
4. When all of the group members have received their crackers, the trainer randomly selects one participant to begin the introductions. The participant then eats the two crackers and introduces himself or herself. When he or she has finished the introduction, the trainer randomly selects another group member. Again that member eats his or her crackers and immediately introduces himself or herself to the entire group.
5. The process is continued until all of the group members have eaten their crackers and introduced themselves.

Variations

■ After the introductions, the group leader may give each group member two more crackers. One at a time, the participants must eat their additional crackers and then repeat the other group members' names.

■ After the introductions, the trainer may ask the participants to mill about the room, and, without eating additional crackers, ask one another for more information about themselves.

Trainer's Notes

_____

_____

_____

_____

_____

_____

_____

_____

Slogans That Fit

Activity Summary This exercise asks the participants to select well-known slogans that they feel describe their lives. This structured experience is most appropriate for educational programs or sessions that emphasize personal interaction among group members. This activity is generally more effective when used during the early stage of the group's formation.

Training Application *Time Reference:* Approximately 10 to 15 minutes.
Group Size: Unlimited.
Space Required: A room that contains adequate writing space for all of the participants. The area must be large enough to accommodate the comfortable seating of the group members.
Materials Needed: For each participant, a pencil and a piece of paper.

Trainer Administration
1. While the group leader distributes paper and pencils, the participants are to think about their personal or professional lives.
2. The trainer then asks that each group member write down three famous slogans, sayings, or lines of poetry that seem appropriate for describing his or her personal life or professional career. For example: "The early bird catches the worm" may describe a participant who likes to be prepared, while "Do unto others as you would have them do unto you" may reflect another group member's personal philosophy.
3. When the participants have completed this task, the trainer asks for a volunteer to share his or her slogans with the entire group. The process continues until all of the group members have read the quotations that they have chosen.
4. The group leader may then wish to initiate a general discussion on how personal philosophies affect professional behavior.

Variations ■ The trainer may instruct the group members to form pairs and then share their slogans with their partners. After the pairs have discussed their slogans, the trainer reassembles the large group. The partners then share with the entire group the information they have obtained from one another.

- The group leader may ask each participant to choose a partner. After the partners have spent 10 minutes interviewing one another, each participant then writes three slogans that he or she feels describe his or her partner's personal or professional life.

Trainer's Notes

Spelling Bee

Activity Summary

This exercise introduces the participants to one another by having them act as letters of the alphabet and then spell one another's names. This activity is generally more effective when used in the early stage of the group's formation.

Training Application

Time Reference: Approximately 10 to 15 minutes.

Group Size: Best suited for a group of 20 to 25 participants.

Space Required: A room that is large enough to permit the unrestricted movement of the learners.

Materials Needed: For each participant, a straight pin and a trainer-prepared piece of paper with a letter of the alphabet printed on it; for the trainer, a roster of the participants' names. The group leader should prepare pieces of paper for all of the letters in the alphabet except Q, X, and Z; the letters must be large enough to be seen clearly at a distance of 15 feet. If the group contains more than 23 participants, the trainer can either repeat the entire alphabet or prepare additional pieces of paper which have vowels written on them. If the group contains fewer than 23 participants, two or more letters must be given to some or all of the participants. (In this case members with identical letters should follow one another in accordance with the instructions of the activity.)

Trainer Administration

1. The trainer begins this exercise by telling the participants that they will be becoming acquainted with one another by acting as letters of the alphabet.
2. The group leader then gives each participant a straight pin and a piece of paper with a letter of the alphabet written on it. The group members are instructed to pin the papers to their chests.
3. Next the trainer explains that each person in the group is going to introduce himself or herself by first name.
4. Referring to a roster, the group leader calls out a name. The person whose name is to be formed then calls out the letters in his or her name.

5. The participants having the letters that appear in the name go to the front of the room and line up to spell the name (see example #1 of Sample Names). If the name contains a double letter or repeats the same letter (and there are not enough participants who have the same letter), the person with the letter must move back and forth in the line to show where the letter appears in the name (see example #2 of Sample Names). If one person is responsible for more than one letter appearing in the name, he or she must move back and forth holding up the appropriate letter in the appropriate space.

Sample Names

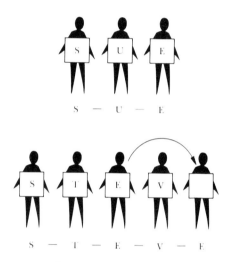

6. The process is repeated until the names of all of the participants have been called out and then formed.

Variations ■ The trainer may request that, instead of names, the participants spell out words that relate to the topic of the training session or program. For example: "efficient," "sales," "supervisor," etc.
■ The group leader may not call out the names but may ask each participant to spell his or her name. Thus, the name is not known until the line has formed, and the participant has given all of the letters in his or her name.

■ If the group is large enough, the trainer can ask the participants to line up and spell out the first and last names of each group member.

Trainer's Notes

_____

_____

_____

_____

_____

_____

_____

_____

Wanted Posters

Activity Summary This exercise asks the participants to introduce themselves through Wanted Posters they have prepared. This activity is generally more effective when used in the early stage of the group's formation.

Training Application

Time Reference: Approximately 15 to 20 minutes.

Group Size: Best suited for a group of 10 or more participants.

Space Required: A room that contains adequate writing space for all of the participants. The area must be large enough to permit the unrestricted movement of the learners.

Materials Needed: For each participant, a straight pin, a pencil, and a copy of the prepared Wanted Poster (see the last page of this exercise).

Trainer Administration

1. The trainer explains that the group members will be introducing themselves through Wanted Posters that they create about themselves.
2. The group leader then gives each participant a straight pin, a pencil, and a copy of the Wanted Poster.
3. The participants are given five minutes in which to complete the posters and pin them to their backs.
4. Next the trainer tells the group members to stand and then mill around the room, reading each other's Wanted Posters and sharing their own posters with others.
5. The group leader may process the activity by reassembling the group and then initiating a discussion on self-perceptions.

Variations

■ The trainer may ask the group members to pair off and then make posters for each other.
■ The group leader may request that, instead of pinning their posters to their backs, the participants tape them to the walls of the room. Then the group members walk around and read one another's posters.

Trainer's Notes

_____

_____

_____

_____

_____

_____

_____

_____

_____

WANTED POSTER

W A N T E D

Name —————————————————

Occupation ——————————————

For

Always being—————————————

———————————————————

Having strong needs for ——————————

———————————————————

Greatly valuing ————————————

———————————————————

Living by the slogan ————————————

———————————————————

———————————————————

What's in a Name?

This exercise asks the participants to pair off and then create as many words as they can from the letters in their partner's name. This activity is generally more effective when used in the early stage of the group's formation.

**Training
Application**

Time Reference: Approximately 15 to 20 minutes.

Group Size: Unlimited.

Space Required: A room that has the potential for flexible seating. The area must be large enough to permit the unrestricted movement of the learners.

Materials Needed: For each participant, a pencil and a piece of paper; for the trainer, masking tape.

**Trainer
Administration**

1. The trainer explains that the participants will be involved in an exercise that is designed to help them become better acquainted with one another.
2. The group leader asks the participants to stand and look around the room. Each of them is then to select a partner whom he or she would like to get to know.
3. While the trainer gives each participant a pencil and a piece of paper, the partners are to sit facing each other and then perform brief introductions of themselves.
4. Next the group leader instructs each participant to write his or her partner's first, middle, and last names at the top of the piece of paper.
5. The trainer then tells the participants that they have five minutes in which to create as many words as possible out of the letters in their partners' names.
6. When the allotted time has elapsed, the partners share their lists with each other.
7. The trainer then asks the entire group to form a circular seating arrangement with the partners sitting next to each other. The participant who has formed the most words from his or her partner's name begins by introducing his or her partner; the partner then introduces him or her. The introductions may include a sampling of the words created from the letters in the partner's names.

8. The introductions continue around the circle until all of the partners have presented each other to the entire group.
9. The trainer may conclude the activity by asking the participants to sign their word lists and then tape them on the wall for others to see.

Variations

■ If the group contains fewer than 20 participants, the trainer may wish to conduct the activity as a large-group exercise. The group leader writes one participant's first, middle, and last names on a blackboard or on a piece of newsprint taped to the wall. For one minute the group members brainstorm all of the words that they can create from that participant's name. The process is repeated for all of the participants' names.

■ The group leader may ask the participants, working individually, to form as many words as possible from their own names. The group members then introduce themselves briefly to the entire group and tell how many words they have created.

Trainer's Notes

_____

_____

_____

_____

_____

_____

_____

_____

Word Associations

This exercise uses word associations to pair off the participants. This activity is generally more effective when used in the early stage of the group's formation.

Time Reference: Approximately 20 to 25 minutes.

Group Size: Best suited for a group of 10 to 20 participants.

Space Required: A room that is large enough to permit the unrestricted movement of the learners.

Materials Needed: For each participant, a piece of masking tape and a trainer-prepared piece of paper with a word printed on it in large letters (see Word Associations List on the last page of this exercise).

1. While giving each participant a strip of masking tape and a piece of paper with a previously selected word printed on it, the trainer explains that the group members will be pairing off by using word associations. (If the group contains an uneven number of participants, the trainer will need to take part in the exercise or a three-part association should be prepared. For example: William Jennings Bryan, Tom, Dick, and Harry, etc.)
2. While the participants tape their papers to their chests, the trainer explains that each of their words matches or complements another word. For example: bread matches butter (see Word Associations List).
3. Each participant is then given a short period of time to find his or her partner. The associated pairs are then to spend five minutes learning about each other's personal and professional lives.
4. When the allotted time has elapsed, the trainer reassembles the group, and the partners are then responsible for briefly introducing each other to the entire group.

■ The trainer may choose word associations that are all subject related. For example: associations involving food, famous couples, well-known books and their authors, characters and popular television shows or movies, etc.

■ The trainer may use word associations that are more difficult to match. For example: bedroom and house, rustic and scenic, time and motion, grapes and wine.

Trainer's Notes

_____

_____

_____

_____

_____

_____

_____

WORD ASSOCIATIONS LIST

1. Ham and eggs
2. Ice cream and cake
3. Pork and beans
4. Soup and crackers
5. Liver and onions
6. Peanut butter and jelly
7. Key and lock
8. Pilot and airplane
9. Ocean and waves
10. Hammer and nail
11. Joe Namath and football
12. Romeo and Juliet
13. Sampson and Delilah
14. Edgar Allen Poe and "The Raven"
15. Leonardo da Vinci and "Mona Lisa"
16. Dag Hammarskjöld
17. Barbra Streisand
18. Fred Astaire and Ginger Rogers
19. "Butch Cassidy and the Sundance Kid"
20. Archie and Edith Bunker

OPENERS AND
WARM-UPS

Openers and Warm-Ups

Extremely versatile by design, opener and warm-up activities can be used in a wide variety of settings. The icebreakers in this division loosen inhibitions by stimulating, challenging, and motivating the participants. Developed to heighten the creative resources of the group, these activities often elicit intense, playful interaction. The group leader may use openers and warm-ups to begin a program, start a session, prime the group after a break, ready the learners for new content material, or shift the focus of study.

The success or failure of these activities depends, in part, upon the group leader, for he or she must establish a climate that gives the participants permission to "let their hair down." The leader can quickly develop this climate through the use of subtle yet important behaviors. Voice inflection, gestures, body posture, eye contact, and verbal instructions all signal a tone that the group members receive and interpret quickly. A tone signaling that it is appropriate to try new behaviors, explore the unknown, engage in playful behavior, and think spontaneously will foster the participants' creative exploration.

Openers and warm-ups, like some of the other types of icebreakers, can be used to examine such aspects of communication as consensus seeking, problem solving, and nonverbal interaction. Participants often discover that the information being studied is made clearer because of their direct and immediate experience during an icebreaker. A program on leadership, for example, may be bolstered by the learnings derived from the participants' roles as team members during one of the opener or warm-up activities.

When the group leader provides proper encouragement, he or she will find that openers and warm-up icebreakers can provide excellent results, for these activities demonstrate that learning can be both meaningful and enjoyable.

Band Together

This exercise helps the participants reduce their inhibitions as they act as musical instruments. This icebreaker is effective at any time during the learning program.

**Training
Application**

Time Reference: Approximately 10 to 15 minutes.

Group Size: Unlimited.

Space Required: A room that has the potential for flexible seating. The area must be large enough to permit the unrestricted movement of the learners.

Materials Needed: For each participant, a trainer-prepared slip of paper naming a particular musical instrument, such as a violin, piano, cello, flute, trumpet, etc.; for the trainer, a small box, such as a shoe box.

**Trainer
Administration**

1. After asking the participants to form a semicircular seating arrangement, which may have several rows, the trainer explains that the group members will be imitating the various instruments in the world-famous Chicago Symphony.

2. When the participants are in position, the group leader tells each participant to draw from the box a slip of paper naming the musical instrument he or she is to portray.

3. Next the participants are asked to stand and simultaneously imitate their instruments, thus approximating the sounds of musical instruments being tuned before a performance.

4. After instructing the group members to sit down, the trainer then gives them the title of a familiar tune they will be performing together. For example: "Mary Had a Little Lamb," "Three Blind Mice," etc. (The group may be given several songs to "play.")

5. The participants practice "playing" the song, acting and sounding like their particular instruments.

6. After the brief practice, the trainer conducts the participants in a full-group rendition of the chosen song(s).

Variations

■ The trainer may ask each participant to choose the instrument he or she wishes to portray.

■ If the group contains more than 20 participants, the trainer may instruct the participants to set themselves up as an orchestra, with the strings sitting together, the woodwinds together, the percussion instruments together, etc.

Trainer's Notes

_____

_____

_____

_____

_____

_____

_____

Blackboard Sentences

This exercise asks the participants, working in teams, to race against one another to formulate a sentence to which each team member has added a word. This icebreaker is effective at any time during the learning program.

Training
Application

Time Reference: Approximately 7 to 10 minutes.

Group Size: Best suited for a group of 25 or fewer participants. If the group contains more than 25 participants, three teams may be formed.

Space Required: A room that is large enough to permit the unrestricted movement of the learners.

Materials Needed: For each team, a blackboard and a piece of chalk or a sheet of newsprint (taped to the wall) and a marker.

Trainer
Administration

1. The trainer begins by explaining that, working in teams, the participants will be competing to see which team is the first to complete a group sentence.
2. Next the participants are asked to divide into two teams. If the group contains an uneven number, one participant may compete twice.
3. The group leader sets up blackboards for each team or tapes two pieces of newsprint to the wall.
4. The teams are then to line up 10 feet from their blackboards or sheets of newsprint.
5. After giving the first person in each team's line a piece of chalk or a black marker, the trainer explains the rules of the game.
   a. Each of the team members is responsible for adding one word to his or her team's sentence. (If the teams are uneven, one participant will be competing twice.)
   b. The first person in each line is to come forward and write the first word of his or her team's sentence. After doing so, he or she returns to his or her team, gives the chalk or marker to the next player, and then goes to the end of the team's line. (No preplanning of sentences is allowed.)
   c. The next player then comes forward, adds a word, returns to the line, and so on until the

last team member completes the sentence. (The sentence must contain the same number of words as there are members on the team.)

d. A player may not add a word between words that have already been written.

e. The final result must be a full sentence—not a fragment.

f. The winner is the team that is the first to build a full sentence using words contributed by all of its members.

6. After explaining the rules, the trainer gives a signal, and the race begins.

7. The exercise continues until both teams have finished their sentences. The trainer then reads the sentences out loud.

8. The group leader may wish to process the activity with a disucssion on the more serious aspects of the exercise, i.e., the value of anticipatory thinking, the individual cooperating in a group task, etc.

Variations

■ The trainer may tell the teams that all of the words in each team's sentence must begin with some specific letter, such as "B" or "S".

■ The group leader may have the two teams compete against the clock. This will allow the teams to watch each other attempt to build a group sentence. The winner is the team to build a complete sentence in the lesser amount of time.

Trainer's Notes

_____

_____

_____

_____

_____

_____

_____

_____

Charades With Art

Activity Summary

This exercise, a variation of charades, asks the participants to sketch, instead of act out, the words of well-known proverbs. This activity is generally more effective when used during the later stage of the training program or session.

Training Application

Time Reference: Approximately 10 to 20 minutes.
Group Size: Best suited for a group of 10 or more participants.
Space Required: A room that is large enough to permit the unrestricted movement of the learners.
Materials Needed: For each team, a pad of newsprint and several colored markers or crayons; for the trainer, the Sample Proverbs List (see the last page of this exercise).

Trainer Administration

1. The trainer tells the group members that they will be playing a version of charades in which, instead of pantomiming, they will sketch simple pictures or symbols to represent the words in well-known proverbs. The group leader may wish to show the participants a sample sketch of a proverb (see Sample Sketch).

2. The group leader then divides the participants into two teams. The two teams sit at the opposite ends of the room so that each can work with some degree of privacy.

3. Next each team sends a representative to the center of the room. The trainer gives each representative several sheets of newsprint and two or three colored markers or crayons. Both representatives receive slips of paper with the same proverb written on them (see Sample Proverbs List).

4. After explaining to the entire group that the object of the game is to see which team can guess the proverb first, the trainer tells the two teams that the representatives are to return to their respective teams and, without speaking, to draw pictures and symbols that identify the words in the proverb. Their drawings may not contain the actual words or any part of a word that appears in the famous saying (see Sample Sketch).

5. The members of each team then attempt to guess the proverb their representative has drawn.

6. The team to identify the proverb first receives one point. Then both teams send new representatives forward to receive another proverb from the trainer.

7. The exercise continues for 10 minutes or until all of the proverbs have been drawn and identified. The team with the higher number of points is declared the winner.

Sample Sketch

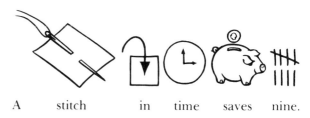

A   stitch   in   time   saves   nine.

Variations

■ Instead of proverbs, the trainer may use the titles of books, songs, and movies or the names of famous people. For example: *Around the World in Eighty Days,* "Moon River," "Bridge over Troubled Water," "Michael Rowed the Boat Ashore," Queen Victoria, Bluebeard, etc.

■ The group leader may request that two representatives from each team work together to draw the same proverb.

■ The trainer may direct the teams to use a combination of art and pantomime. For example: A player may tug on his or her ear to indicate "sounds like" and then draw what the particular word does sound like. For example: To indicate the word "stitch," the player may draw a witch and then tug on his or her ear.

Trainer's Notes

_____

_____

_____

_____

_____

_____

SAMPLE PROVERBS LIST

1. Man cannot live by bread alone.
2. He who laughs last laughs best.
3. A bird in the hand is worth two in the bush.
4. Money is the root of all evil.
5. The early bird catches the worm.
6. People who live in glass houses should not throw stones.
7. Look before you leap.
8. Steady wins the race.
9. Too many cooks spoil the broth.
10. Don't put the cart before the horse.

Debate

This exercise asks the participants to test their ability to talk continuously. This icebreaker is effective at any time during the learning program.

Training Application

Time Reference: Approximately 15 to 20 minutes.
Group Size: Unlimited, but best suited for a group of 10 or more participants.
Space Required: A room that has the potential for flexible seating. The area must be large enough to permit the unrestricted movement of the learners.
Materials Needed: None.

Trainer Administration

1. The group leader begins by asking the participants to form a circular seating arrangement.
2. When the group members are seated, the trainer explains that they will be participating in a mini-debate that is designed to test their ability to talk without stopping.
3. The trainer solicits two volunteers and asks them to come to the center of the circle. The volunteers are quickly to choose some topic or issue and decide which side of the issue each of them will debate. The topic may be serious or humorous in nature. For example: "The Pros and Cons of Nuclear Energy" or "The Choice Between Hard and Soft Mattresses."
4. The trainer then explains the rules for the debate.
   a. The debate is to last for two minutes, during which time each debater is to attempt to convince the other of his or her side of the issue.
   b. The debaters must face each other at all times.
   c. The debaters may use gestures as they speak.
   d. Most importantly, the debaters are to speak at the same time, and they are to talk continuously.
   e. The winner will be the participant who hesitates the least during the debate. The rest of the group members will decide who wins, although they may, if necessary, declare a draw.
5. After explaining the rules, the trainer signals the beginning of the debate and then calls a halt when two minutes have elapsed. When the group members have determined the outcome, the exercise

is repeated with two different volunteers debating a different topic. The process continues with as many debaters as time allows.

Variations
■ The group leader may ask that the volunteers use no gestures during their debate.
■ The trainer may secretly assign the same side of an issue to both debaters.
■ The group leader may ask four participants, two for each side of an issue, to debate at one time. Each participant would try to make the others hesitate in their delivery.

Trainer's Notes

_____

_____

_____

_____

_____

_____

_____

First Impressions

This exercise asks the participants to record their first impressions of persons depicted in photographs and to share these impressions with the group. This icebreaker is effective at any time during the learning program, but it is most appropriate for educational programs or sessions that emphasize personal interaction among group members.

Training Application

Time Reference: Approximately 10 to 15 minutes.

Group Size: Unlimited, but best suited for a group of 20 or fewer participants.

Space Required: A room that is large enough to accommodate the comfortable seating of the participants.

Materials Needed: For each participant, a pencil and a piece of paper; four numbered photographs that show individuals in action or at rest. (The photographs may be chosen from newspapers or magazines; the selected pictures should contain a mixture of portraits and action shots.)

Trainer Administration

1. The trainer states that in this exercise the participants will be asked to record and then share their first impressions of other people.
2. After giving each participant a pencil and a piece of paper, the trainer explains that the group members will be looking at four numbered pictures of individuals. As the participants view each photograph, they are to record the number of the picture and then write a label and a descriptive statement that indicate their first impression of what the person in the photograph is like and what he or she is doing. The trainer reminds the participants that they are not to talk to each other until they have responded to all four pictures.
3. The trainer then holds up the first picture and, if necessary, moves around the room until all of the participants have viewed the photograph clearly. When the group members have recorded their impressions, the trainer displays the second picture. The process continues until the participants have reacted to all four photographs.

4. The group leader then asks the participants to share their impressions of the photographs with the entire group. After the participants have compared and contrasted their responses, the trainer may wish to conclude the exercise with a general discussion on the impact of initial impressions and perceptions.

Variation   ■ The trainer may ask the group members to interpret pictures that depict scenes instead of people. The group discussion then centers on how and why individuals react differently to the same experience.

Trainer's Notes

_____

_____

_____

_____

_____

_____

_____

_____

Gossip

This exercise uses a familiar game, Gossip, as a warm-up for the participants. This icebreaker is effective at any time during the learning program.

**Training
Application**

Time Reference: Approximately 5 to 10 minutes.

Group Size: Unlimited, but best suited for a group of 10 to 20 participants. If the group contains more than 20 participants, subgroups should be formed.

Space Required: A room that has the potential for flexible seating.

Materials Needed: For the trainer, the Sample Rumors Sheet (see the last page of this exercise).

**Trainer
Administration**

1. The trainer asks the group members to form a circular seating arrangement.
2. When the participants are seated, the trainer tells them that they will be playing a familiar game, Gossip.
3. The group leader then explains how the game will be played. The sender must whisper the rumor clearly, but he or she cannot repeat the rumor if the listener has not heard it correctly.
4. The trainer begins the game by whispering one rumor in the ear of the person sitting to his or her right and then another rumor in the ear of the person to his or her left (see Sample Rumors Sheet).
5. Both rumors continue around the circle; the last persons to receive them must repeat what they have heard. The original rumors are then read to the entire group.
6. Using the group's Gossip game as the example, the trainer initiates a discussion of rumors and how they can be distorted.

Variations

■ If the group contains more than 20 members, the trainer may ask for 10 volunteers to leave the room. The remaining participants all receive written copies of the rumor. Then the volunteers are called into the room one at a time. The trainer reads the rumor to the first person, the first person calls in a second person and repeats (based upon

memory) the rumor to him or her, and so on until all of the volunteers are back in the room.
■ The group leader may solicit a volunteer to serve as the head of the circle. The volunteer makes up his or her own rumor, writes it down for reference at the end of the activity, and then begins the gossip. After this round the game is repeated with a new person creating the rumor. Two or three rounds will usually be played.

Trainer's Notes

_____

_____

_____

_____

_____

_____

_____

SAMPLE RUMORS SHEET

RUMOR #1

Bob said that he came to the picnic only because his boss, Fred, told him that Carol's boss, Steve, was sending all of his people and he did not think Bob should be left out because his future promotion might be affected.

RUMOR #2

Three days ago I heard that the plans for the new plant were lost one day before they were due. The cover-up took place with almost uncanny organization so that just three hours before the presentation took place, six team members were able to duplicate the 12-page report from scratch and no one knew except the two people I overheard discussing the situation.

Grin and Bear It

Activity Summary

This exercise asks the participants to play a game in which they attempt to make one another smile. This icebreaker is effective at any time during the training program.

Training Application

Time Reference: Approximately 10 to 15 minutes.
Group Size: Unlimited.
Space Required: An area that is large enough to permit the unrestricted movement of the learners.
Materials Needed: None.

Trainer Administration

1. The trainer begins by explaining to the group members that they will be engaging in an activity that is enjoyable and energizing.
2. The group members are then asked to divide into two teams. If the group contains an uneven number, one participant may serve as a judge.
3. The trainer instructs the groups to stand and line up so that all members of one team are directly across from the members of the other team.
4. A toss of the coin determines which team plays first.
5. The trainer then explains the rules of the game.
   a. The members facing each other, referred to as "opponents," take turns trying to make each other smile.
   b. The first two opponents are to make faces or use body actions as they attempt to make one another smile. They may not, however, use verbal communication.
   c. The person who smiles or grins first must remove himself or herself from the group.
   d. A draw is declared if neither smiles after two minutes, and the two opponents remain on their respective teams.
   e. The second set of opponents then repeats the process until a winner or a draw is declared.
   f. The trainer and extra person (if there is one) will watch closely to determine who has or has not grinned. After all of the team members have competed, or after 10 minutes, the team with the larger number of members is declared the winner.
6. At a signal, the first opponents begin the battle.

Variations
- If the group contains 10 or fewer members, the trainer may instruct the participants to find partners. One at a time the pairs come to the front of the entire group, and the partners take turns trying to make each other smile.
- The group leader may tell the participants that they may use verbal communication, as well as body movements and facial expressions, to make their opponents laugh.

Trainer's Notes

_____

_____

_____

_____

_____

_____

_____

_____

_____

Hear! Hear!

Activity Summary

This exercise asks the participants to give impromptu speeches while their fellow group members provide vigorous audience reaction. This activity is generally more effective when used during the later stage of the training program or session.

Training Application

Time Reference: Approximately 15 to 20 minutes.
Group Size: Unlimited, but best suited for a group of 10 or more participants.
Space Required: A room that has the potential for flexible seating.
Materials Needed: None.

Trainer Administration

1. The trainer first asks the participants to arrange their chairs in several rows and to sit facing the front of the room.
2. The group leader then explains that the participants will be giving brief impromptu speeches while their fellow group members give them vigorous positive reinforcement.
3. Next a volunteer is solicited to come forward and stand facing the group. The volunteer is to give a two-minute impromptu speech on a subject of his or her choosing. If the group members appear anxious, the trainer may consider giving the first speech.
4. Before the volunteer begins, the trainer tells the other participants to watch the speaker carefully. When the speaker gestures with his or her left hand, the group members are to applaud. When the speaker raises his or her right hand, the group must yell "Hear! Hear!" When the speaker gestures with both hands, the group must yell and applaud at the same time.
5. After telling the volunteer to use as many appropriate gestures as possible during his or her speech, the trainer signals the volunteer to begin the exercise.
6. After two minutes a new volunteer is solicited, and the gesture-response pattern is repeated.
7. The activity continues for 15 minutes or until the entire group seem's "charged up."

Variation ■ As each new speaker comes forward, the trainer may change the responses the group members must make for each of the speaker's gestures.

Trainer's Notes

_____

_____

_____

_____

_____

_____

_____

_____

Hello

Activity Summary

This exercise asks the participants each to create a special "hello" for other participants to repeat. This activity is generally more effective when used in the early stage of the group's formation.

Training Application

Time Reference: Approximately 5 minutes.

Group Size: Best suited for a group of 25 or fewer participants.

Space Required: A room that has the potential for flexible seating. The area must be large enough to permit the unrestricted movement of the learners.

Materials Needed: None.

Trainer Administration

1. The trainer begins by asking the group members to form a large, circular seating arrangement.
2. When the participants are seated, the group leader tells the group members that this exercise will help them begin the training session or program in an unusual manner.
3. Next the trainer explains that one at a time each participant is to stand, take two steps toward the center of the circle, and say "hello!" The participant is to use facial expression(s), and/or particular movement(s) of his or her hands, body, legs, etc. to create and then emphasize his or her special "hello" to the group. After each "hello," the other group members are to stand, take two steps forward, and return the "hello," repeating the participant's gestures and facial expressions.
4. The group leader gives the first "hello," which is then repeated by the entire group. The person sitting to the leader's right then gives his or her "hello," and the process is repeated until all of the participants have given and received their special greeting.

Variations

■ The group leader may give several greetings for the group members to repeat.

■ The trainer may ask each participant to give his or her name during the "hello." For example: A participant nods his head, smiles broadly, waves both hands, and says, "Hello, my name is Jack

Martin"; the group repeats his motions and calls out, "Hello, Jack!"

_____

_____

_____

_____

_____

_____

_____

_____

I Bequeath

**Activity
Summary**

This exercise involves the participants in the writing
of group wills. This icebreaker is effective at any
time during the learning program.

**Training
Application**

Time Reference: Approximately 15 to 20 minutes.
Group Size: Best suited for a group of 10 to 20 participants.
Space Required: A room that has the potential for flexible seating.
Materials Needed: For each participant, a pencil and
a piece of paper; for the trainer, a blackboard and
chalk or a piece of newsprint and a black marker.

**Trainer
Administration**

1. The group leader asks the participants to form a
circular seating arrangement.
2. When the group members are seated, the trainer
explains that they will be writing group wills—in
case they "die of boredom" during the training
session.
3. After giving each participant a pencil and a piece
of paper, the trainer tells the group members to
fold their paper in an accordian style so that the
paper is divided into five sections (see Accordian-
Style Fold illustration). In the first section, the
participants are to write their names. They then
fold the first section down and pass the paper to
the person sitting to their right.
4. In the second section of the folded paper they
have received, the participants write some item or
possession that they wish to bequeath to someone.
They then fold the section down and pass the
paper to their right.
5. In the third section, the participants write the
name of the person sitting to their left. They again
fold the paper down and pass it on to their right.
6. In the fourth section, the participants write the
purpose or reason for their bequest, fold the paper, and pass it to their right.
7. In the fifth section, the participants write a condition they wish to attach to their bequest.
8. While the participants are completing step #7, the
trainer writes the following on a blackboard or on
a piece of newsprint: _____ hereby wills and

bequeaths ————— to ————— for the purpose of (or in order that) ————— on condition that —————.

9. The trainer then solicits a volunteer from the group. The volunteer reads the will he or she has in hand, inserting the information from each fold into its appropriate space on the trainer's blank will form. The exercise continues until all of the participants have read their wills.

Accordian-Style Fold

| Karen Jones |
| mink coat |
| Bob Tanner |
| it may grow and multiply |
| he lives in it throughout the year |

Variations

■ The group leader may ask the participants to perform this exercise legitmately; that is, each group member writes a will that emphasizes the personal traits he or she would like to leave behind.

■ After the exercise has been completed, the trainer initiates a discussion in which the participants tell how they would like others to remember them.

Trainer's Notes

_____

_____

_____

_____

_____

_____

_____

I Expect

Activity Summary

This exercise asks the participants to reveal their expectations of the training program, of each other, and of themselves. This structured experience is most appropriate for educational programs or sessions that emphasize personal interaction among group members. This activity is most effective when used during the early stage of the group's formation.

Training Application

Time Reference: Approximately 10 to 15 minutes.

Group Size: Best suited for a group of 10 to 20 participants.

Space Required: A room that is large enough to accommodate the comfortable seating of the participants.

Materials Needed: For each participant, a pencil and a piece of paper.

Trainer Administration

1. After distributing paper and pencils to all of the group members, the trainer asks each participant to write down the following statements: "From the leader of this session, I expect _____," "From the other participants in this session, I expect _____," and "From myself in this session, I expect _____."
2. The group members are then given five minutes in which to complete the statements.
3. When the allotted time has elapsed, the trainer collects the papers. Then, without revealing the participants' identities, the group leader reads all of the completed statements out loud.
4. The trainer may then initiate a brief discussion of the participants' expectations and how these expectations are to be met during their time together.

Variations

■ The group leader can list the participants' responses on three sheets of newsprint headed "Expectations of the Trainer," "Expectations of Others," and "Expectations of Myself." The resulting lists would be posted so that the group members could refer to them during the training session.

■ The trainer can use other incomplete statements. For example: "I want _____," "I need _____," and "I wish that _____."

Trainer's Notes

_____

_____

_____

_____

_____

_____

_____

_____

Identifying Touch

This exercise challenges the participants' sense of touch as they attempt to identify a series of small objects placed in paper bags. This icebreaker is effective at any time during the trainer program.

**Training
Application**

Time Reference: Approximately 10 to 15 minutes.

Group Size: Best suited for a group of 12 or more participants.

Space Required: An area that has the potential for flexible seating. The room must contain adequate writing space for all of the participants.

Materials Needed: For each participant, a pencil and a piece of paper; for each subgroup, a paper bag containing 10 small objects, such as an apple, a balloon, an eraser, a sponge, a necktie, a paper clip, a rolled-up newspaper, a straw, an envelope, and a piece of chalk. (The objects may vary for each subgroup.)

**Trainer
Administration**

1. The trainer tells the group members that they will be playing a game that is designed to challenge their sense of touch.

2. The group leader then divides the participants into groups of four or five and asks the members of each subgroup to sit together at one of the tables in the room.

3. Next the trainer gives each participant a pencil and a piece of paper and each subgroup a bag containing six small objects. The group leader tells the subgroup members that they are not to look into the bags.

4. The group leader explains that one at a time each subgroup member is to close his or her eyes, reach into the subgroup's bag, and feel the objects with his or her right hand. The participnats may not remove the objects from the bag. (No talking is permitted during this stage of the activity.) Then the subgroup member is to remove his or her hand from the bag, and, without looking at or feeling the objects again, write on a sheet of paper the identity of each object. (A participant is only allowed one exposure to the bag's contents.)

5. The next subgroup member then closes his or her eyes and attempts to identify the objects by using his or her sense of touch. The process is repeated until all of the subgroup members have felt and then tried to identify the objects.
6. The subgroup members conclude the exercise by opening the bag, taking out the objects, and checking to see how many objects each of them has identified correctly. Discussion among subgroup members is now allowed.

Variations

■ The trainer may ask that all of the subgroup members feel the objects and then as a group decide on the identity of each item in the bag.

■ The group leader may give each subgroup a rubber glove. The subgroup members wear the glove and thus must use their forearms to identify the objects.

■ The trainer may have the subgroups compete against each other if identical objects are in each subgroup's bag. After all of the members of the subgroup have touched the objects, the subgroup as a whole attempts to reach a consensus on the contents of the bag. The subgroup that identifies correctly the greatest number of objects is declared the winner.

Trainer's Notes

_____

_____

_____

_____

_____

_____

_____

_____

Imagination

Activity Summary

This exercise uses the participants' ability to think creatively as they respond to some unusual questions. This activity is generally more effective when used during the later stage of the training program or session.

Training Application

Time Reference: Approximately 5 to 10 minutes.

Group Size: Unlimited, but best suited for a group of 10 to 20 participants.

Space Required: A room that is large enough to accommodate the comfortable seating of the participants.

Materials Needed: For the trainer, the Imagination List (see the last page of this exercise).

Trainer Administration

1. The trainer asks the group members to let their minds expand as they consider innovative ways of thinking and perceiving.
2. Next the group leader explains that in this exercise the participants will be asked to respond to some questions and then to explain why they responded as they did.
3. The trainer begins the exercise by choosing a group member at random and asking him or her a question from the Imagination List. When the group member has given his or her response and has provided a rationale for the answer, the trainer may ask another participant to answer the same question or a different question from the Imagination List.
4. When all of the participants have responded to at least one question, the group leader may wish to process the exercise and its relevance to problem solving, brainstorming, or the examination of basic assumptions. During the discussion the trainer will need to keep in mind the goals for processing as outlined in the Trainer's Introduction.

Variations

■ If the group contains more than 20 participants, the trainer may divide the participants into smaller groups in which the members ask each other questions from the Imagination List.

- After giving copies of the Imagination List to all of the participants, the group leader may ask them to form pairs. The partners then take turns asking and answering the questions.
- The trainer may request that all of the participants write down their responses to each of the questions and then share their answers with the group either verbally or by posting them on the wall of the room.

Trainer's Notes

_____

_____

_____

_____

_____

_____

_____

_____

IMAGINATION LIST

1. What color is the letter "S"?
2. What does happiness look like?
3. What color is today?
4. What does purple taste like?
5. What does your self-image sound like?
6. What texture is the color green?
7. What color is the smell of your favorite perfume?
8. What does love look like?
9. What is your favorite sense?
10. What color is your favorite song?
11. What texture is your favorite scent?
12. What does winter sound like?
13. What sex is the number 6?
14. How old is the letter "P"?
15. How does the letter "M" feel?
16. What color is the fragrance of soap?
17. What does a cloud sound like?
18. What is the weight of your anger?
19. What is the shape of your imagination?
20. What does your favorite book feel like?

Knots

Activity Summary
This exercise has the participants, holding hands in a large circle, entangle and then untangle themselves in accordance with one group member's instructions. This structured experience is most appropriate for educational programs or sessions that emphasize personal interaction among group members. This activity is generally more effective when used during the early stage of the group's formation.

Training Application
Time Reference: Approximately 5 to 10 minutes.

Group Size: Unlimited, but best suited for a group of 20 or fewer participants. If the group contains more than 20 participants, two subgroups should be formed.

Space Required: An unobstructed area without tables or chairs.

Materials Needed: None.

Trainer Administration
1. The group leader first asks the participants to stand, form a circle, and then join hands.
2. When the group members are in position, the trainer explains that they will be taking part in an exercise in which they must cooperate with one another and follow one person's instructions carefully.
3. Next the trainer solicits a volunteer to serve as a problem solver. The volunteer is then asked to leave the room.
4. Next the trainer asks the participants to walk over and/or under one another's joined hands so that the group becomes tightly entangled. At no time during this activity are the group members to let go of one another's hands.
5. When the participants are completely entangled, the trainer asks the volunteer to return to the room and begin to unwind the group members without causing them to unclasp their hands.
6. The exercise continues until the group members, with their hands still joined, are again standing in a large circle.

Variations
■ If the group members appear to be daring, the trainer may ask them to wear blindfolds during

the initial entangling. When the volunteer returns to the room, the group leader removes the participants' blindfolds.

■ The group leader may give the volunteer two or three minutes in which to untangle the group. If he or she cannot do so within the allotted time, the group members, without letting go of one another's hands, untangle themselves.

Trainer's Notes

_____

_____

_____

_____

_____

_____

_____

_____

Laugh

Activity Summary
This exercise employs structured laughter to help the participants feel more comfortable with one another. This icebreaker is effective at any time during the learning program.

Training Application
Time Reference: Approximately 10 to 15 minutes.
Group Size: Unlimited.
Space Required: An unobstructed area without tables or chairs.
Materials Needed: A balloon, a beanbag, a halfdollar, or any other small object.

Trainer Administration
1. The trainer asks all of the group members to stand up and form a circle.
2. When the participants are in position, the group leader stands in the middle of the circle and tells them that they will be taking part in an activity that is designed to make them feel more comfortable with one another.
3. The trainer then solicits a volunteer to come to the middle of the circle. The group leader shows the participants an object and explains that when the volunteer tosses this object into the air, they are all to laugh out loud continuously. When the object lands on the floor, the participants must immediately stop laughing. The person who does not stop laughing, as judged by the trainer, must stand in the center of the circle and throw the object into the air. (The original volunteer remains in the center of the circle as do all of the participants who are caught laughing after the object has landed on the floor.)
4. The volunteer tosses the object, and the activity begins. The exercise continues until everyone is laughed out or called into the middle of the circle.

Variations
■ The trainer may penalize the group member who cannot stop laughing when the object lands on the floor. For example: The participant may have to bark through the next toss of the object, or he or she may be forbidden to laugh at all during the rest of the exercise.

■ The group leader may tell the participant in the center of the circle to toss the object and laugh while the other group members remain silent. Any group members who laugh trade places with the participant in the middle of the circle and thus become the ones who toss the object.

Trainer's Notes

_____

_____

_____

_____

_____

_____

_____

Number Groups

Activity Summary

This exercise asks the participants to form groups quickly, the number of participants in each group being based on a number that is called out. This icebreaker is effective at any time during the learning program.

Training Application

Time Reference: Approximately 5 to 10 minutes.
Group Size: Best suited for a group of 12 or more participants.
Space Required: An unobstructed area without tables or chairs.
Materials Needed: None.

Trainer Administration

1. The trainer tells the group members that they will be taking part in an exercise that demands quick thinking.
2. The group leader begins the activity by explaining that when a number is called out, the participants must form groups that contain that number of people.
3. The numbers are to be called quickly, and the participants must move rapidly to form their groups. For example: "Form groups of 4 . . . form groups of 7 . . . form groups of 4."
4. If a person cannot find a group, then he or she is responsible for calling out the next number.
5. The exercise continues for 5 to 10 minutes.

Variations

■ The group leader may have the participants wear blindfolds during the activity. They therefore must rely on their sense of touch to determine the number of people in each of the groups they are asked to form.
■ The trainer may ask the group members to form "even numbered" or "odd numbered" groups. The group leader may even say, "Form groups that contain multiples of the number 4" or "Form groups of 6 minus 2 members."

Trainer's Notes

**Trainer's
Notes**
continued

_____

_____

_____

_____

_____

_____

Patchwork Fiction

Activity Summary This exercise asks the participants to put together a group story composed of sentences that have been clipped from various newspapers and magazines. This icebreaker is effective at any time during the learning program.

Training Application

Time Reference: Approximately 10 to 15 minutes.

Group Size: Unlimited, but best suited for a group of 10 or more participants.

Space Required: A room that is large enough to permit the unrestricted movement of the learners.

Materials Needed: A box filled with sentences that the trainer has clipped from newspapers and magazines. The trainer's selection of sentences should be as diverse as possible. For example: a piece of dialogue from a cartoon, a sentence from an editorial, a slogan from an advertisement.

Trainer Administration

1. The trainer informs the participants that they will be creating a story for the group to submit to a well-known periodical for publication in its next issue.

2. The group leader then displays a box that is filled with sentences he or she has clipped from newspapers and magazines. Each participant is to draw a sentence from the box.

3. Next the trainer instructs the group members to read their sentences out loud as they walk around the room. The group members then are to work together to form a group story that makes some sense. They have five minutes in which to perform this task. (All of the group members' sentences must be used in the story.)

4. When they have planned their story, the participants then line up, standing in the order in which their sentences are to appear in the finished story.

5. After the group members have lined up in sequence, the participant with the first line in the story reads his or her sentence out loud, the person with the next line reads his or her sentence, and so on until the entire story has been presented.

■ The trainer asks the participants to divide into work groups of six to eight members each and to put together a patchwork story by pasting or taping their sentences on newsprint. The group members then add lines to the story to make it more creative and to provide transitions between the sentences.

■ Following step #4 in the Trainer Administration section, the group leader may tell the participants that when they read their sentences out loud, they are to insert their names or the name of one of their fellow group members in the place of any proper name that appears in their sentence. They may also be asked to substitute the name of the city or training site for every city or place named in their sentences.

■ The trainer may request that the participants write a sentence about what they did over the past weekend. The trainer collects these sentences, places them in the box, and thus incorporates them into the group story the participants will create by following the steps in the Trainer Administration section.

Trainer's Notes

_____

_____

_____

_____

_____

_____

_____

_____

Problems and Solutions

Activity Summary

This exercise asks the participants to write questions and answers on different pieces of paper and then, by trading answers, to come up with unusual solutions. This icebreaker is effective at any time during the learning program.

Training Application

Time Reference: Approximately 10 to 15 minutes.

Group Size: Unlimited, but best suited for a group of 10 to 20 participants.

Space Required: A room that is large enough to accommodate the comfortable seating of the participants.

Materials Needed: For each participant, a pencil and two pieces of paper; for the trainer, an empty box, such as a shoe box.

Trainer Administration

1. The trainer begins by explaining that the participants are going to solve the problems that they consider to be important.

2. After giving each group member a pencil and two sheets of paper, the trainer asks the participants to write a problem question on one of their sheets of paper. The question may be personal, such as "What can be done about my family's irritability in the morning?" or it may be more political or social, such as "How can the country of India solve its problem with poverty?"

3. When the participants have written their questions, the group leader requests that on their second sheet of paper they each record a solution to their chosen problem. After folding their papers so that no one can read them, the group members place the solutions in a box held by the trainer. They are to keep the papers upon which they have written their problem questions.

4. Next the trainer walks around the room and has each group member select a new solution from the box. (The group members are not to look at the solutions until the trainer instructs them to do so.)

5. When all of the participants have new solutions, the group leader solicits a volunteer to read his or her question out loud. The volunteer then

opens the new solution and reads it to the group. For example: "The problem is 'What can be done about my family's irritability in the morning?'; the solution is 'Require the people to take birth control pills.'"

6. The exercise continues until all of the participants have shared their problem questions and new solutions.

Variations
■ The group leader can ask that the participants direct their problems and solutions toward work-related topics.

■ The trainer may request that the group members exchange solutions instead of drawing them out of a box.

■ The group leader may ask the participants to place their problem questions in the box. The trainer then reads each question out loud and at random calls on a participant to share his or her solution with the group.

Trainer's Notes

_____

_____

_____

_____

_____

_____

_____

_____

Profiles

Activity Summary This exercise asks the participants to draw profiles of themselves to share with the group. This activity is most effective when used during the early stage of the group's formation.

Training Application *Time Reference:* Approximately 10 to 15 minutes.

Group Size: Best suited for a group of 10 to 20 participants.

Space Required: A room that contains adequate writing space for all of the participants.

Materials Needed: For each participant, a pencil and a large piece of drawing paper.

Trainer Administration

1. After giving each participant a pencil and a piece of drawing paper, the trainer tells the group members that in this exercise they will attempt to identify one another by profile only.
2. Next the group leader asks the participants to spread out so that each of them has some privacy in which to work.
3. Then the trainer explains that each participant is to draw his or her own profile. The drawing should be a side view in which the group member has, to the best of his or her ability, depicted his or her head and shoulders.
4. The participants are then given five minutes to complete their drawings.
5. When the allotted time has elapsed, the group leader collects the profiles and puts them face down on a table (or on the floor).
6. Next the trainer solicits a volunteer to come forward and, at random, select one of the profiles. The volunteer holds up the profile so that the other group members can view it clearly. The group members (or, if requested to do so, the volunteer) then attempts to identify the person by the profile the individual has drawn.
7. The process is repeated until all of the profiles have been examined and identified.

Variations ■ The trainer may privately ask some participants to draw profiles of specific group members rather than of themselves.

■ The group leader may ask the participants to form pairs. The partners draw profiles of each other that they then share with the entire group.

Trainer's Notes

_____

_____

_____

_____

_____

_____

_____

_____

_____

Progressive Poetry

This exercise asks the participants, working in small groups, to write poems. This icebreaker is effective at any time during the learning program.

Time Reference: Approximately 15 to 20 minutes.
Group Size: Best suited for a group of 12 to 20 participants.
Space Required: A room that has the potential for flexible seating.
Materials Needed: For each work group, a pencil and a piece of paper.

1. The trainer begins the activity by asking the group members to divide into work groups of four participants each. If necessary, a work group may contain five members.
2. When the work groups have formed, the trainer explains that the members of each group will be working together to write a poem.
3. The group leader gives one person in each group a pencil and a piece of paper and tells him or her to fold the paper in an accordian style so that the paper contains eight sections.
4. The trainer then explains the exercise:
   a. Each group's poem is to contain two four-line stanzas.
   b. Each member of the group is to write a line for each stanza in the work group's poem.
   c. The participant who folded the paper is to begin the poem by writing a sentence in the first space on his or her work group's piece of paper. (Other group members should not observe or be told what is being written.)
   d. Next the participant is to fold back his or her line and, telling only the last word of the first line of the work group's poem, pass the pencil and paper to the next group member.
   e. That group member then writes his or her line, making sure that the last word of the line rhymes with the last word of the first line of the poem. He or she repeats only the last word of the second line to the next participant, who then writes the third line of poem, again making sure that the last word of his or her line

rhymes with the last word of the line that precedes it.

   f. When the fourth person has completed the stanza by adding his or her line, the group begins the second stanza with a different group member providing the stanza's first line.

5. After explaining the exercise, the trainer directs the work groups to begin their poems and tells them they have 10 minutes in which to create their literary masterpieces.

6. When the allotted time has elapsed, the trainer asks a volunteer from each group to stand and read his or her group's poem to all of the participants.

Variations

■ If the group contains more than 30 participants, the trainer can expand the size of the work groups and increase the length of the poems. For example: A group of 40 participants may divide into work groups of eight members each; the work groups write poems consisting of four four-line stanzas.

■ The trainer may request that the group members rhyme lines 1 and 3 and then lines 2 and 4, or lines 1 and 2 and then lines 3 and 4 of a stanza. In this case the participant who writes a line tells the last word to the person who must rhyme with the line he or she has written.

■ The trainer may give every other group member a word to use as the last word in his or her line. For example: first writer, second writer ("moon"), third writer, fourth writer "loon"), etc. Each participant writes his line on a separate piece of paper. The trainer collects the papers in order and then reads the poem to the entire group.

Trainer's Notes

_____

_____

_____

_____

_____

_____

Proverbial Shout

This exercise uses proverbs in a guessing game that serves as a group warm-up. This icebreaker is effective at any time during the learning program.

Time Reference: Approximately 5 to 10 minutes.
Group Size: Unlimited, but best suited for a group of 10 to 20 participants.
Space Required: A room that is large enough to accommodate the comfortable seating of the participants.
Materials Needed: None.

1. The trainer explains that the participants will be taking part in an exercise that is designed to help them become more comfortable with one another.
2. The group leader then solicits a volunteer and asks him or her to leave the room. When the volunteer has left, the trainer asks the rest of the group members to choose a proverb. For example: "He who laughs last laughs best."
3. When the group members have chosen a proverb, the trainer assigns each word of the saying to a different participant. For example: Six participants are needed for the six words in the sample proverb. The rest of the participants choose one, possibly humorous-sounding word, such as "armadillo."
4. The trainer tells the group members that when the volunteer returns to the room, they are to shout out their particular word simultaneously and continuously. The volunteer's task will be to sort out the words and put together the proverb.
5. The trainer then brings the volunteer back into the room and, without identifying the proverb or the group's chosen word, repeats the instructions to him or her (see steps #3 and #4). At a signal from the trainer, the group members begin shouting their words while the volunteer attempts to piece together the proverb that the participants have chosen.
6. The exercise may be repeated with different volunteers as many times as the group would like,

allowing approximately two to three minutes for each repetition.

7. The group leader may process the exercise in terms of achieving an understanding of open communication or establishing communication guidelines for the training session or program.

Variations
■ The trainer may conduct the exercise as a contest, with two volunteers (or two teams of volunteers) competing against each other to guess the proverb in the least amount of time.

■ The group leader can use this exercise to help the participants become acquainted. Members of the group trade names to shout out, and the volunteer must try to match the right person to the correct name.

Trainer's Notes

_____

_____

_____

_____

_____

_____

_____

_____

Solemn and Silent

This exercise asks the participants to remain solemn and silent for as long as they can. This icebreaker is effective at any time during the learning program.

Time Reference: Approximately 10 to 15 minutes.
Group Size: Best suited for a group of 10 to 20 participants.
Space Required: A room that has the potential for flexible seating. The area must be large enough to permit the unrestricted movement of the learners.
Materials Needed: None.

1. The trainer explains that the participants will be playing a game that requires self-control.
2. Next the group leader asks the participants to pair off and then stand back-to-back with their partners.
3. At a signal from the trainer, the partners are to face each other, look one another in the eye, and try to remain solemn and serious. The partners are not to speak.
4. The object of the exercise is to see which of the partners can remain solemn for the longer period of time.
5. When one of the pair laughs, the "solemn one" then joins a new partner who has won the solemn award in the match with his or her first partner. As the losers of the first round watch, the winners repeat the exercise. Again the process is repeated until the two most solemn group members meet in head-to-head competition.
6. The activity continues until only one person still has not laughed. That person is declared the "Solemnest."

■ The trainer may conduct the activity as a contest in which teams of players compete against each other. A team loses any player who laughs during a "showdown" between two opposing team members.

_____

_____

_____

_____

_____

_____

_____

_____

Uncle Fred's Suitcase

Activity Summary

This exercise challenges the participants to remember the items they have packed into an imaginary suitcase. This icebreaker is effective at any time during the learning program.

Training Application

Time Reference: Approximately 5 to 10 minutes.
Group Size: Best suited for a group of 10 to 20 participants.
Space Required: A room that has the potential for flexible seating.
Materials Needed: None.

Trainer Administration

1. The trainer asks the group members to form a circular seating arrangement.
2. When the participants are seated, the group leader explains that they are going to take part in an exercise that is designed to stimulate their creativity and challenge their memories: they are going to pack Uncle Fred's suitcase.
3. The trainer solicits a volunteer and tells him or her to begin the exercise by saying "I packed Uncle Fred's suitcase with _____" and then naming some item or object. For example: "I packed Uncle Fred's suitcase with ballet shoes." The person sitting to the right of the volunteer is to repeat what the volunteer has said and then to add his or her item. Objects or items cannot be repeated.
4. The exercise continues around the circle as each participant recites the previous items and then adds another object to Uncle Fred's suitcase. Group members may help any participant who cannot remember some object that has been named.
5. When the last participant in the circle has repeated the items and has added his or her item to the list, the trainer asks the entire group to stand and recite what is in the suitcase: "I packed Uncle Fred's suitcase with _____, _____, _____, _____, etc."

Variations

■ The trainer may instruct the group members to say "I am here to _____" and then complete the thought with a descriptive word or phrase, such as "have fun," "learn," "experience something new," etc. Each participant repeats the phrases used before him and then adds his or her own descriptive word(s).

■ The group leader may handle the exercise as a contest in which the volunteer's chair serves as the head of the circle. If a participant forgets any item, he or she still adds an object but then goes to the end of the circle. The end is the chair to the right of the head chair. All of the other participants behind that member move up one chair to the right. The activity continues around the circle for five minutes.

Trainer's Notes

_____

_____

_____

_____

_____

_____

_____

_____

Vegetable Sing

Activity Summary This exercise asks the participants to harmonize the names of vegetables. This activity is generally more effective when used during the later stage of the training program or session.

Training Application

Time Reference: Approximately 5 to 10 minutes.
Group Size: Unlimited, but the larger the group, the better.
Space Required: A room that is large enough to permit the unrestricted movement of the learners.
Materials Needed: None.

Trainer Administration

1. The group leader asks the participants to divide into three groups.
2. When the groups have formed, the trainer explains that the entire group will be harmonizing the names of vegetables.
3. Group 1 is to sing soprano; group 2 is to sing alto and tenor; group 3 is to sing bass.
4. The trainer tells group 3 to practice singing the word "tomatoes" in a high key; group 2 is to sing the word "potatoes" in an alto/tenor key, while group 3 is to practice singing the word "goulash" in the bass key.
5. The groups disperse to practice singing their words, each group locating an area in which its member can have some degree of privacy.
6. After several minutes, the trainer, who will be serving as conductor, calls the groups together and explains that on the count of three, all of the groups are to sing out their words in their respective keys. The groups then practice their harmony. If the harmony is atrocious, the trainer asks the work group(s) to find a new key.
7. The group leader then raises a hand and conducts: "1—2—3." The exercise concludes when the groups have produced what the trainer feels to be an acceptable harmony.

Variations

■ The group leader may assign the soprano key to the male participants and ask the women to sing alto and bass.

■ The trainer may divide the participants into three groups and ask them to hum in harmony to a specific, well-known tune.
■ The group leader may use other words for the harmonies. For example: "cold beer," "iced tea," and "lemonade."

Trainer's Notes

_____

_____

_____

_____

_____

_____

_____

_____

Who Am I?

Activity Summary This exercise asks the participants to identify the names of famous persons. This activity is generally more effective when used in the early stage of the group's formation.

Training Application *Time Reference:* Approximately 15 to 20 minutes.
Group Size: Unlimited, but best suited for a group of 10 to 20 participants.
Space Required: A room that is large enough to permit the unrestricted movement of the learners.
Materials Needed: For each participant, a trainer-prepared sheet of paper with the name of a famous person written on it; masking tape and pencils.

Trainer Administration
1. The trainer begins by explaining that in this exercise the participants will be asked to identify the names of famous persons.
2. The group leader then tapes to the back of each participant a piece of paper with the name of a famous person written on it. The group member is not to see what is taped on his or her back.
3. The trainer then tells the group members that each of them now has a new identity. Their task is to find out who they are.
4. The participants are to mill around the room and simultaneously to ask each other questions that can be answered with "yes" or "no." For example: "Am I living?" "Am I a film star?" "Have I ever been on the cover of a famous magazine?" "Have I ever or do I now work in the field of science?"
5. If the participant receives a "yes" answer, he or she can continue to ask that group member questions until a "no" response is given. When the participant receives a "no" response, he or she must move to another group member to ask another question.
6. The trainer explains that when a group member has established his or her new identity, he or she is to remove the tag, write his or her name across the top of the paper, and then tape the tag to his or her chest. The participant may then mill around the room, helping other group members discover their identities.

7. The exercise concludes when all of the participants have discovered who they are.

Variations

■ The trainer may request that the participants seek to learn their identities by asking fellow group members to describe the famous person's personal or professional strengths and weaknesses. For example: A participant may ask a fellow group member to describe a personal strength, and the group member may respond with "This person is (was) very sexy," while a request for a personal weakness might be answered with "This person is (was) extremely insecure." (Famous person: Marilyn Monroe)

■ The trainer may ask the participants to act out nonverbally the characteristics of each other's new identity. For example: To help a group member identify former President Eisenhower, a participant might smile broadly while pretending to swing a golf club.

Trainer's Notes

_____

_____

_____

_____

_____

_____

_____

_____

Professional Development Topics

Unlike the other icebreakers in this encyclopedia, the professional development exercises focus on specific themes that are commonly encountered in business, industry, education, health care, and other human service organizations. The activities in this division can be used for educational programs or for presentations on supervision, time management, motivation, problem solving, leadership, stress, salesmanship, or assessment.

The following icebreakers are most effective when, at the completion of the activity, the group leader spends some time discussing the participants' reactions to the structured experience. By exploring such areas as assumptions, values, attitudes, and perceptions, the leader will maximize his or her flexibility for leading into or illustrating whatever course material is to follow.

Some of the icebreakers in this division will elicit responses that pertain to the participants' present work settings. To ensure confidentiality, it is recommended that the group members do not use real names when they are referring to others outside the learning group itself. In addition, the group leader may wish to remind the participants of other general groundrules for honoring the confidentiality of others: information of a personal nature is not to be shared outside the group; specific individuals outside the group should not be discussed without their permission; and information of a personal nature should only be shared on a voluntary basis.

Although somewhat different in design, professional development icebreakers still maintain the same basic function as the other activities in this reference text. When selected carefully and executed competently, these exercises will reduce the group members' inhibitions, lower the barriers between participants, and shift the energy level of the group itself. Like other icebreakers, these activities are appropriate for beginning a training program, starting individual sessions, or renewing interest after a break or lull period.

A Supervisor's Dilemma

Activity Summary This exercise presents a case discussion through which the participants may examine various supervisory styles. This icebreaker is effective at any time during the learning program.

Training Application

Time Reference: Approximately 25 to 30 minutes.

Group Size: Unlimited, but best suited for a group of 12 to 20 participants.

Space Required: A room that has the potential for flexible seating.

Materials Needed: For each participant, a copy of the Supervisor's Dilemma Sheet (see the last page of this exercise).

Trainer Administration

1. The trainer begins by explaining that in this exercise the group members will use a case discussion to examine various supervisory decisions.

2. After giving each participant a copy of the Supervisor's Dilemma Sheet, the trainer tells the group members to read the case discussion carefully and then to choose one or two options that they see as viable solutions to the given problem.

3. After five minutes the group leader asks the participants to form work groups of four members each and to discuss with their fellow group members the options they have chosen and the rationales for their selection. Each work group is then to attempt to reach a consensus on the most appropriate option.

4. After 10 minutes the trainer calls the participants together and asks each work group to report on its selection. The group leader then initiates a discussion on supervisory styles, using the various options for the case discussion as examples to illustrate differences.

Variations

■ The group leader may ask the entire group to reach a consensus on one option for solving the given problem.

■ The trainer may request that the participants, working individually and drawing upon their own professional experiences, write case discussions and options. (No real names are to be used.) Volunteers then present their cases and options for the entire group to discuss.

Trainer's Notes

_____

_____

_____

_____

_____

_____

_____

SUPERVISOR'S DILEMMA SHEET

Steven is the supervisor of a five-man team assigned to the Production Department of a large manufacturing facility. Several of the team members have told him that two other team members have formed an amorous liaison outside of work. Although Steven has not totally substantiated the existence of the relationship, he intuitively feels that it is affecting the team's morale and the two individuals' dedication to their jobs.

As supervisor, what should Steven do?

1. Overlook the situation.
2. Fire the two individuals.
3. Bring the situation up at a team meeting.
4. Confront the two by calling them in for separate conferences.
5. Sabotage the relationship.
6. Let the couple know that he will be monitoring their work and will be documenting any abuses.
7. Have team-building sessions to improve the entire group's morale.
8. Call the other team members in and ask for their input.
9. Bring the two team members in together to discuss the issue.
10. Quickly establish a policy of no fraternizing outside of work.

Arrange the Cartons

Activity Summary This exercise asks the participants to evaluate a task performance that has been based on extremely vague directions. This icebreaker is effective at any time during the learning program.

Training Application

Time Reference: Approximately 10 to 15 minutes.

Group Size: Unlimited.

Space Required: A room that is large enough to accommodate the comfortable seating of the participants.

Materials Needed: For each participant, a pencil and a copy of the Data Sheet (see the last page of this exercise).

Trainer Administration

1. While distributing pencils and copies of the Data Sheet to all of the group members, the trainer explains that this exercise asks them to evaluate an individual's performance of a specific task.
2. The participants are then to read the Data Sheet and, in accordance with the instructions on the sheet, to rate each arrangement of the cartons.
3. When the group members have completed their required ratings, the trainer solicits volunteers to share their results and rationales with the entire group.
4. The group leader then leads a discussion that focuses on the evaluation of job performance: the assumptions followed, the variations in the perceptions of a task, the criteria used in performance evaluation, the relationship between given instructions and end results, etc.

Variations

■ The group leader may ask the participants to rank, order the possible arrangements of the cartons (1 indicating the most effective organization, and 5 indicating the least effective arrangement).

■ The trainer may divide the participants into two groups. The members of each group create evaluation problems for the members of the other group to solve.

**Trainer's
Notes**

_____

_____

_____

_____

_____

_____

_____

_____

_____

DATA SHEET

Bill has been given the responsibility of arranging or rearranging 10 cartons in the company's supply room. His supervisor tells him to "straighten them so we can have access to the cartons—and be neat about it."

Following are examples of the ways in which Bill could arrange the cartons. Considering your interpretation of the instructions Bill received, rate each of the arrangements on its fulfillment of the supervisor's directions (1 indicating poor arrangement, and 5 indicating very effective arrangement).

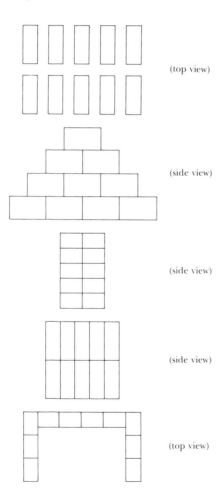

(top view)

(side view)

(side view)

(side view)

(top view)

Assessing Performance

Activity Summary

This exercise asks the participants to list and then set priorities on general methods for assessing performance. This icebreaker is effective at any time during the learning program.

Training Application

Time Reference: Approximately 25 to 30 minutes.

Group Size: Best suited for a group of 12 to 20 participants.

Space Required: A room that has the potential for flexible seating.

Materials Needed: For each participant, a pencil and a piece of paper.

Trainer Administration

1. After explaining that in this exercise the group members will be asked to examine methods for assessing performance, the trainer asks the participants to break into discussion groups of four or five members each.

2. When the groups have formed, the trainer gives each participant a pencil and a piece of paper and then explains that the members of each discussion group are to work together to brainstorm *general* methods for assessing job performance. (In other words, how does one go about effectively evaluating an individual's specific responsibilities?) Each group is to list on paper its chosen general methods of assessment. The groups may wish to address specifically such areas as criteria selection, means of observation, data collection, strategies for accuracy checks, etc.

3. After 15 minutes or when the groups have finished their brainstorming, the trainer asks each discussion group to set priorities on the methods its members have listed by rank ordering their items.

4. When the discussion groups have completed this task, the group leader reassembles the large group. A volunteer from each discussion group then shares his or her group's findings with the entire group.

Variations

■ The trainer may ask the participants to work individually to complete the exercise, or the group leader may conduct the activity with the entire group instead of breaking the participants into subgroups.

■ The trainer may select a type of job that is relevant to the group members' professions (i.e., production manager, comptroller, division supervisor, factory line worker, etc.) and have the work groups focus on specific methods or ways for assessing the performance of that particular job.

Trainer's Notes

_____

_____

_____

_____

_____

_____

_____

_____

Brainstorming

Activity Summary

This exercise challenges the participants, working individually and then in groups, to brainstorm solutions to a given problem. This icebreaker is effective at any time during the learning program.

Training Application

Time Reference: Approximately 25 to 30 minutes.
Group Size: Best suited for a group of 12 to 20 participants.
Space Required: A room that has the potential for flexible seating.
Materials Needed: For each participant, a pencil, a piece of paper, and a copy of the Madison Avenue Sheet (see the last page of this exercise).

Trainer Administration

1. The trainer first tells the participants that in this exercise they will examine first the individual and then the group problem-solving process as they brainstorm solutions to a given problem. The group leader may want to explain that in brainstorming a person or a group of people writes down every possible idea, solution, approach, etc. without regard to feasibility, practicality, etc.

2. Next the group leader gives each participant a pencil, a piece of paper, and a copy of the Madison Avenue Sheet. Working individually, the participants then spend 10 minutes brainstorming as many possible solutions as they can and then recording these solutions on their sheets of paper. During this time each participant should attempt to become more aware of his or her own problem-solving processes.

3. After 10 minutes the group leader asks the participants to form work groups of four persons each and to spend five minutes brainstorming additional solutions to the same problem. As they work, the group members should take note of the group problem-solving process.

4. The trainer then reassembles the group and asks the participants to compare the number of solutions arrived at in the individual and in the group problem-solving efforts.

5. The exercise may then conclude with a discussion

in which the group members share their feelings about individual and group problem-solving efforts.

Variations   ■ The trainer may present two different problems, one for the individual process and one for the group problem-solving process.
■ The group leader may begin the exercise with group problem solving and then have the participants brainstorm individually.
■ The trainer may ask the group members to share their solutions orally or to post their lists for all of the participants to read.

Trainer's Notes

MADISON AVENUE SHEET

A New York store that specializes in lingerie has been suffering a significant decline in sales during the past year. Management is unsure about the cause(s) of this loss except that it may be due to more aggressive marketing by its competitors (large numbers of direct-mail advertisements, more ad space in the *New York Times,* more costly window displays, etc.) Since the store is unable to secure additional funds for marketing, its management has decided to find new ways to increase the store's marketing efforts without spending more money.

You have been brought in as a consultant to assist in the expansion of the store's viability and hence increase its sales. How is this to be done?

_____

_____

_____

_____

_____

Buyer's Guide

This exercise challenges the participants to create Buyer's Guides that they feel accurately describe themselves. This activity is generally more effective when used in the early stage of the group's formation.

Time Reference: Approximately 25 to 30 minutes.
Group Size: Unlimited, but best suited for a group of 12 to 20 participants.
Space Required: A room that has the potential for flexible seating.
Materials Needed: For each participant, a pencil and a copy of the Buyer's Guide Sheet (see the last page of this exercise).

1. While giving each participant a pencil and a copy of the Buyer's Guide Sheet, the trainer explains that self-knowledge is a very important factor in effective management.
2. The group members then are given five minutes in which to fill out their Buyer's Guide Sheets on themselves. The group leader encourages the participants to be as creative as possible in completing this task.
3. Next the group leader divides the participants into groups of four or five members each. The members of each work group then have 15 minutes in which to share their Buyer's Guide Sheets with one another.
4. When the allotted time has elapsed, the trainer reassembles the group and solicits volunteers to read their creative self-profiles out loud.
5. After a number of participants have shared their Buyer's Guide Sheets, the trainer may process the exercise through a group discussion on the relationship between self-knowledge and effective management.

■ The trainer may request that each participant fill out a Buyer's Guide Sheet on his or her ideal self.
■ The group leader may ask the participants to form pairs. The partners then fill out Buyer's Guide Sheets for each other. (This variation requires that

the group members be acquainted with one another.) The trainer then leads a general discussion on perceptions and effective management.

Trainer's Notes

_____

_____

_____

_____

_____

_____

_____

_____

BUYER'S GUIDE SHEET

Standard features: _____

_____

Additional options: _____

_____

Performance record: _____

_____

Maintenance requirements: _____

_____

Direct benefits of ownership: _____

_____

Comparison to competitors' models: _____

_____

Carrot or Stick?

**Activity
Summary** This exercise asks the participants to examine and then rank order a list of motivating factors that relate to the professional environment. This icebreaker is effective at any time during the learning program.

**Training
Application** *Time Reference:* Approximately 25 to 30 minutes.
Group Size: Unlimited, but best suited for a group of 12 to 20 participants.
Space Required: A room that has the potential for flexible seating.
Materials Needed: For each participant, a pencil and a copy of the Carrot and Stick Sheet (see the last page of this exercise).

**Trainer
Administration** 1. While giving each group member a pencil and a copy of the Carrot and Stick Sheet, the trainer tells the participants to think about the motivating factors that are important to them in their work environments.
2. The participants are then to examine closely the items listed on the Carrot and Stick Sheet. After considering each item and its relationship to himself or herself and to his or her work environment, each group member is to rate the items in their perceived order of importance (1 indicating highest priority, and 10 showing lowest priority).
3. After five minutes the trainer directs the participants to divide into work groups of four members each and to discuss their ratings with their fellow group members.
4. After 10 minutes the trainer reassembles all of the participants and leads a discussion on the findings of the work groups.

Variations ■ The trainer may ask the participants to work in groups of four or five members each and within their groups to attempt to reach a consensus on the rank ordering of the items on the Carrot and Stick Sheet.
■ The group leader may request that each participant share with the entire group the rationale for his or her ratings.

■ The trainer may direct the group to come up with a list of motivating influences that are then listed on a blackboard or newsprint pad. Next the group members attempt to reach a consensus on the rank ordering of the items.

Trainer's Notes

_____

_____

_____

_____

_____

_____

_____

_____

CARROT AND STICK SHEET

_____ Dental plan; cost-of-living raise, 20 days of paid vacation each year.

_____ Strokes from the boss; strokes from peers; strokes from unexpected sources, such as ex-consumers or business rivals.

_____ Promotion; compensation time; overtime.

_____ Excellent starting salary; guaranteed three-month raise; annual promotions.

_____ Good personnel evaluation; merit raise; ongoing recognition for work done well.

_____ Educational benefits; pension plan; stock-option plan.

_____ Piped-in music; large, private office space; impressive title.

_____ Four 15-minute breaks; one-hour lunch break; personal leave time.

_____ Grievance committee; union; good relationship with boss.

_____ Ability to yield power; creative professional options; increased responsibility.

Coping with Stress

Activity Summary This exercise asks the group members each to describe their primary source of work-related stress and then to develop strategies for coping with this stress factor. This icebreaker is effective at any time during the learning program.

Training Application *Time Reference:* Approximately 25 to 30 minutes.
Group Size: Unlimited.
Space Required: A room that has the potential for flexible seating.
Materials Needed: For each participant, a pencil and a piece of paper; for the trainer, a blackboard and chalk or a pad of newsprint and a black marker.

Trainer Administration

1. The group leader begins by explaining that in this exercise each participant will be examining his or her primary source of stress in his or her present work setting and then developing a means for coping with it more effectively. Before proceeding further, the trainer may wish to discuss the positive and negative aspects of stress.
2. After giving each group member a pencil and a piece of paper, the trainer asks each participant to describe on paper the one source of stress that most commonly interferes with his or her work-related tasks. (In the event that a source of stress is an individual, no name should be used.)
3. When all of the participants have completed their descriptions, the trainer collects the papers and informs the group members that they will be pooling their experiences to explore ways of coping with interfering stress factors more effectively.
4. The group leader then quickly scans the participants' sheets and chooses one item that appears to be representative of a common stress factor. Without revealing the author of the description, the group leader reads the item out loud, and the group members then spend two minutes brainstorming possible strategies for coping with this stress factor. The trainer should quickly list all suggestions on the blackboard or newsprint.
5. The group members then spend another two

minutes rank ordering the suggestions (1 indicating the most effective strategy). If, within two minutes, a consensus cannot be reached, the trainer can have the group members vote to determine the rank ordering of particular strategies.

6. The group leader then selects another stress factor from the participants' descriptions. The process is repeated until all of the items have been discussed or until the allotted time for the exercise has ended.

7. The trainer may process the activity by encouraging the participants to express their reactions to the experience and then initiating a discussion on stress and additional strategies for coping with it more effectively.

Variations

■ The trainer may divide the group members into discussion groups of four members each. The members of each group then examine one another's primary stress factors and develop strategies for coping with them more effectively. When the discussion groups have completed this task, they return to the large group and share their strategies and/or insights.

■ The group leader may ask that each participant devise his or her own strategy for coping with his or her primary stress factor. After each participant shares his or her stress factor and strategy with the entire group, the rest of the group members offer their suggestions or alternative strategies.

Trainer's Notes

_____

_____

_____

_____

_____

_____

_____

_____

Creative Management

This exercise asks the participants, working in groups, to write booklets on creative management. This icebreaker is effective at any time during the learning program.

**Training
Application**
Time Reference: Approximately 25 to 30 minutes.
Group Size: Best suited for a group of 10 to 20 participants.
Space Required: An unobstructed area containing one table for each work group. The room must be large enough to permit the unrestricted movement of the learners.
Materials Needed: For each work group, five or six sheets of newsprint, a stapler, and a selection of colored markers.

**Trainer
Administration**
1. First the group leader asks the participants to break into work groups of four to five members each.
2. When the work groups have formed, the trainer gives each group five or six sheets of newsprint, a stapler, and enough colored markers for all of the group members.
3. The group leader then explains that each work group is, within 15 minutes, to develop a booklet on creative management. After telling the participants that they are to be as creative as possible in preparing their booklets, the trainer lists the essential elements each booklet must contain: a title, chapter titles, a brief synopsis of each chapter, and a bibliography.
4. The groups then disperse to their work areas and have 15 minutes in which to produce their booklets.
5. When the allotted time has elapsed, the trainer calls the groups together and asks them to share their booklets with all of the participants.

Variations
■ The trainer may give the work groups a free hand in deciding what material to include and how to arrange the information in their booklets.
■ The group leader may ask each participant to create his or her own booklet.

■ The trainer may request that the group members create pictorial booklets on creative management.

Trainer's Notes

_____

_____

_____

_____

_____

_____

_____

Creative Team Building

Activity Summary This exercise challenges the participants, working in groups, to create team-building exercises. This activity is generally more effective when used during the later stage of the training program or session.

Training Application *Time Reference:* Approximately 25 to 30 minutes.

Group Size: Best suited for a group of 10 to 20 participants.

Space Required: An unobstructed area, without tables or chairs, that is large enough to permit the unrestricted movement of the learners. Several small meeting rooms or areas that provide private or semi-private interaction are also needed.

Materials Needed: None.

Trainer Administration
1. The group leader begins by dividing the participants into work groups of four or five members each (depending on the size of the total group).
2. When the groups have formed, the trainer explains that the group members will be taking part in an activity that will challenge their creativity. Each work group is to create an exercise or a game that the work group's members feel will promote or build group spirit.
3. After explaining that the game or exercise should be less than five minutes in length and that it should involve all of the participants, the trainer tells each work group to find an area where its members can work with some degree of privacy. The work groups have five minutes in which to devise their creative, team-building activities.
4. When the allotted time has elapsed, the trainer calls the work groups together. Each work group then leads the entire group in its team-building game or exercise.
5. After all of the work groups have presented their team builders, the trainer may process the exercise through a discussion of the types of activities, attitudes, and behaviors that promote cooperative efforts in the work environment.

Variations ■ The trainer may ask the entire group, or separate individuals, to create a series of team-building exercises or games.
■ The group leader may ask the participants to create nonverbal team-building exercises.

Trainer's
Notes

_____

_____

_____

_____

_____

_____

_____

Effective Employee

Activity Summary

This exercise challenges the participants to record the qualities they feel an effective employee should possess. This icebreaker is effective at any time during the learning program.

Training Application

Time Reference: Approximately 25 to 30 minutes.

Group Size: Unlimited, but best suited for a group of 20 or fewer participants.

Space Required: A room that has the potential for flexible seating.

Materials Needed: For each participant, a pencil and a piece of paper.

Trainer Administration

1. While giving each participant a pencil and a piece of paper, the trainer asks the group members to think about the general qualities they feel an effective employee must possess.

2. The participants are then given three minutes to list these qualities on paper.

3. Next the trainer asks that each group member rank order the items on his or her list according to the perceived importance of each quality (1 representing the most important quality that an employee can possess).

4. When the participants have finished their rank orderings, the trainer asks them to divide into discussion groups of four or five participants each. The members of each discussion group are to share their lists and the rationales for their selections and then attempt to reach a consensus on the five most important qualities they feel an effective employee must possess. (If a consensus cannot be reached within 10 minutes, the group members may vote to determine the group's list of ʹ qualities.)

5. After 10 minutes the trainer calls the discussion groups together and asks a volunteer from each group to read his or her group's top five qualities out loud.

6. When all of the discussion groups have presented their lists, the trainer may process the exercise through a group discussion on the similarities and differences among the various lists. The discussion

should also explore the assumptions, values, and attitudes associated with each group's selection.

Variations ■ The group leader may ask the participants to rate themselves, on a scale of 1 to 10 (1 indicating complete competence, and 10 showing no competence), on how they feel they meet each of their own top five qualities.

■ After the discussion groups report on their lists, the trainer may give the entire group five minutes to reach a final consensus on the top five qualities an effective employee must possess.

Trainer's Notes

_____

_____

_____

_____

_____

_____

_____

_____

Good Supervisor/Manager

Activity Summary

This exercise challenges the participants to describe the qualities a good supervisor/manager must possess. This icebreaker is effective at any time during the learning program.

Training Application

Time Reference: Approximately 25 to 30 minutes.

Group Size: Unlimited, but best suited for a group of 20 or fewer participants.

Space Required: A room that has the potential for flexible seating.

Materials Needed: For each participant, a pencil and a copy of the Good Supervisor/Manager Sheet (see the last page of this exercise); for each discussion group, a copy of the Good Supervisor/ Manager Sheet.

Trainer Administration

1. The trainer begins by explaining that in this exercise the group members will be identifying the qualities they feel a good supervisor/manager must possess.

2. After giving each participant a pencil and a copy of the Good Supervisor/Manager Sheet, the trainer asks the group members, working individually, to fill out the sheets.

3. When the group members have completed this task, they divide into discussion groups of four or five participants each. Next the members of each group share their individual responses with one another.

4. The trainer then gives each discussion group a Good Supervisor/Manager Sheet and explains that each group must now complete the sheet, its members attempting to reach a consensus on the qualities an effective supervisor/manager must have if he or she is to perform competently.

5. After 15 minutes or when the groups have completed their sheets, the trainer asks them to come together. A representative from each group then reads his or her group's Good Supervisor/Manager Sheet to the entire group.

Variations

■ The trainer may have the group members focus on the qualities of poor supervision/management.

(The Good Supervisor/Manager Sheet would need to be modified accordingly.)

■ The group leader may ask the participants to share specific examples that illustrate the characteristics of the good supervisor/manager.

Trainer's Notes

GOOD SUPERVISOR/MANAGER SHEET

1. A good supervisor/manager has the following qualities:

    a. _____

    b. _____

    c. _____

    d. _____

    e. _____

2. A good supervisor/manager expects his or her employees to:

    a. _____

    b. _____

    c. _____

    d. _____

    e. _____

3. A good supervisor/manager never:

    a. _____

    b. _____

    c. _____

    d. _____

    e. _____

Individual Goal Setting

Activity Summary

This exercise asks the participants to set short- and long-term professional goals. This icebreaker is effective at any time during the learning program.

Training Application

Time Reference: Approximately 20 to 25 minutes.

Group Size: Unlimited.

Space Required: A room that has the potential for flexible seating.

Materials Needed: For each participant, a pencil and a copy of the Goal-Listing Sheet (see the last two pages of this exercise).

Trainer Administration

1. While giving each participant a pencil and a copy of the Goal-Listing Sheet, the trainer asks the group members to think about their professional goals.

2. Next each participant is to record his or her daily, weekly, monthly, and yearly professional goals on the Goal-Listing Sheet. The group members should be encouraged to be as specific as possible in formulating their goals.

3. When all of the group members have completed their lists, the trainer asks them to form pairs and to discuss their goals with their partners.

4. After 10 minutes the group leader calls the participants together and initiates a discussion on goal setting and the establishment of priorities for the accomplishment of the established goals.

Variations

■ The group leader may ask the participants to prepare lists that focus on personal as well as professional goals.

■ If the group members are connected by common work bonds, the trainer may instruct them to establish team goals.

Trainer's Notes

_____

_____

_____

**Trainer's
Notes**
continued

_____

_____

_____

_____

_____

GOAL-LISTING SHEET

DAILY GOALS

1. _____

_____

2. _____

_____

3. _____

_____

4. _____

_____

5. _____

_____

WEEKLY GOALS

1. _____

_____

2. _____

_____

3. _____

_____

4. _____

_____

5. _____

_____

GOAL-LISTING SHEET (continued)

MONTHLY GOALS

1. _____

   _____

2. _____

   _____

3. _____

   _____

4. _____ _____

   _____

5. _____

   _____

YEARLY GOALS

1. _____

   _____

2. _____

   _____

3. _____

   _____

4. _____

   _____

5. _____

   _____

Individual Problem Solving

Activity Summary This exercise challenges the participants, working individually, to examine their own problem-solving processes. This icebreaker is effective at any time during the learning program.

Training Application

Time Reference: Approximately 25 to 30 minutes.
Group Size: Unlimited.
Space Required: A room that is large enough to accommodate the comfortable seating of the participants.
Materials Needed: For each participant, a pencil, a piece of paper, and a copy of the Problem Sheet (see the last page of this exercise).

Trainer Administration

1. Explaining that problem solving is often a very individual process, the trainer tells the participants that each of them will have an opportunity to examine the method he or she follows in solving a particular problem.
2. Next the group leader gives each participant a pencil, a piece of paper, and a copy of the Problem Sheet.
3. After reading the problem outline carefully, each group member, working individually, is to indicate his or her solution(s). Then each participant is to write down, step by step, the process he or she followed in solving the given problem (i.e., goal selection, awareness of options, probable consequences of options, solution selection).
4. When all of the participants have completed their lists, the trainer solicits volunteers to share their problem-solving processes with the entire group.
5. Finally, the trainer has the participants give the probable solutions to which their problem-solving processes have led them.

Variations

■ The trainer may ask that each group member devise a solution to the problem and then backtrack to review his or her problem-solving process.
■ The trainer may instruct the participants, working individually, to construct or devise problems for other group members to solve.

**Trainer's
Notes**

_____

_____

_____

_____

_____

_____

_____

_____

PROBLEM SHEET

The Accounting Department and Inventory Control Department of a medium-size warehousing concern both require access to the company's computers for six hours of each eight-hour working day. In the past the departments have had frequent arguments about computer time, and, as a result, the two department supervisors are currently at loggerheads with one another. The time both departments require cannot be reduced. In addition, a new computer system cannot be brought in for at least 12 more months. The problem must be solved quickly if the company is to run efficiently during its peak season, which begins in two weeks.

You have been hired as a consultant to resolve the problem. What will you do?

_____

_____

_____

_____

Please outline the problem-solving steps you used in formulating a solution for this problem.

_____

_____

_____

_____

Intensive Care

This exercise asks the participants to examine a problem situation and then create options for solving the given problem. This icebreaker is effective at any time during the learning program.

**Training
Application**

Time Reference: Approximately 25 to 30 minutes.

Group Size: Best suited for a group of 12 or more participants.

Space Required: A room that has the potential for flexible seating.

Materials Needed: For each participant, a pencil and a copy of the Case Study Sheet (see the last page of this exercise).

**Trainer
Administration**

1. While giving each group member a pencil and a copy of the Case Study Sheet, the trainer explains that the participants will be developing options for managing a specific problem effectively.
2. Next the group leader tells the participants that, working individually, they have five minutes to read the case carefully and then prepare a list of five feasible options for handling the problem.
3. When they have completed their lists, the participants are instructed to form work groups of four or five members each and to discuss their chosen options with their fellow group members.
4. Following their discussion of individually selected options, the work group members are, within 10 minutes, to reach a consensus on the best means for solving the given problem.
5. The trainer then reassembles the entire group, and a spokesperson from each work group reads his or her group's solution to all of the participants.
6. The group leader may then process the activity through a discussion of problem solving, values, perceptions, etc.

Variations

■ The trainer may ask that one or more volunteers present actual problems for the group to explore. (No real names should be used.)

■ The group leader can employ the basic structure of the activity both in the early and then in the later stage of the group's development. In this way the group members and the trainer will be able to observe and then discuss any changes in their problem-solving and listening skills that appear to be a result of the training program.

Trainer's Notes

_____

_____

_____

_____

_____

_____

_____

CASE STUDY SHEET

Barbara is a supervisor of nursing for the night shift in a 50-bed Intensive Care Unit. While doing her final rounds early one morning, she sees Susan, a licensed practical nurse (LPN), leaning against a wall in a patient's room, apparently dozing. A short while later when Barbara calls the LPN to task, Susan responds, "So fire me. I don't care!" and stalks out of the nurses station.

If you were Barbara, what would you do? (List five feasible options.)

1. _____

2. _____

3. _____

4. _____

5. _____

Job Disclosure

Activity
Summary This exercise asks the participants to explore and then identify those elements that affect their work performance. This icebreaker is effective at any time during the learning program.

Training
Application *Time Reference:* Approximately 25 to 30 minutes.

Group Size: Unlimited.

Space Required: A room that has the potential for flexible seating and that contains adequate writing space for all of the participants. The area must be large enough to permit the unrestricted movement of the learners.

Materials Needed: For each participant, a pencil and a copy of the Performance Variables Sheet (see the last page of this exercise).

Trainer
Administration 1. The group leader begins by explaining that this activity gives the participants an opportunity to examine some factors that influence their performance on the job.

2. After giving each participant a pencil and a copy of the Performance Variables Sheet, the trainer informs the group members that they have five minutes in which to complete the forms to the best of their ability.

3. When the allotted time has elapsed, the group leader asks the participants to pair off and then spend approximately 10 minutes sharing information from their sheets with their partners.

4. The trainer may process the exercise by reassembling the group and initiating a discussion on the factors that the participants feel inhibit and/or promote effective performance in the work environment.

Variation ■ The trainer can use other headings for the Performance Variables Sheet. For example: Why I Am Ideally Suited for My Job—Why My Job Does Not Fit Me or My Short-Term Goals—My Long-Term Goals.

Trainer's Notes

_____

_____

_____

_____

_____

_____

_____

_____

PERFORMANCE VARIABLES SHEET

WHAT MAKES MY JOB EASIER

1. _____

_____

2. _____

_____

3. _____

_____

4. _____

_____

5. _____

_____

WHAT MAKES MY JOB MORE DIFFICULT

1. _____

_____

2. _____

_____

3. _____

_____

4. _____

_____

5. _____

_____

Motivating the Manufacturers

Activity Summary

This exercise asks the participants, working in pairs, to devise several solutions to a particular problem; then the pairs cooperate with other pairs to decide on the one best solution to the given problem. This icebreaker is effective at any time during the learning program.

Training Application

Time Reference: Approximately 25 to 30 minutes.

Group Size: Best suited for a group of 12 or more participants.

Space Required: A room that has the potential for flexible seating.

Materials Needed: For each participant, a pencil and a copy of the Motivation Study Sheet (see the last page of this exercise).

Trainer Administration

1. After explaining that this exercise asks the participants to work together to solve a particular problem, the trainer requests that the group members pair off and then sit with their partners.
2. When the pairs have formed, the group leader gives each participant a pencil and a copy of the Motivation Study Sheet.
3. The trainer then explains that the partners are to work together to come up with a number of feasible solutions to the problem outlined on the Motivation Study Sheet.
4. After 10 minutes the group leader asks the partners to join one other pair. The four team members are to discuss their solutions and then attempt to reach a consensus on one solution that they feel will best solve the problem.
5. When another 10 minutes have elapsed, the trainer calls the group members together and asks each team to report on its solution and the rationale for the solution's selection.
6. The group leader may conclude the exercise with a discussion of the factors that improve morale and motivate employees toward higher productivity.

Variations
- The trainer may conduct the activity as a large-group exercise in which the participants brainstorm various solutions and then attempt to reach a consensus on the best solution to the given problem.
- The group leader may direct the participants to devise a problem which they then attempt to solve as a group.

Trainer's Notes

_____

_____

_____

_____

_____

_____

_____

_____

MOTIVATION STUDY SHEET

A major company that makes ball bearings has been experiencing a morale problem which is evidenced by high turnover and low productivity. The problem became apparent several months ago but has become particularly severe in the past month. Management is having a meeting to devise some feasible solution to the problem.

The company's employees work a 40-hour week and are paid a flat rate for their work. Each employee is expected to make a minimum of 100 ball bearings a week. Although the requisite number of bearings have been made, there is a 25% rate of error that is not attributable to any one employee.

Based on the above information, what would you, as part of the management team, do to improve morale and increase productivity?

_____

_____

_____

_____

_____

Motivation Grid

Activity Summary This exercise challenges the participants to identify and then examine the motivating qualities contained in their work environment. This icebreaker is effective at any time during the learning program.

Training Application *Time Reference:* Approximately 15 to 20 minutes.

Group Size: Best suited for a group of 10 or more participants.

Space Required: A room that has the potential for flexible seating.

Materials Needed: For each participant, a pencil and a blank grid card (a five-by-seven index card) that is marked off into nine sections (see the Completed Sample Grid Card on the last page of this exercise).

Trainer Administration
1. The trainer tells the group members that during this exercise each participant will be identifying and then examining the qualities of his or her work environment that motivate him or her to perform more effectively and/or more efficiently.
2. After giving each participant a pencil and a blank trainer-prepared grid card (see Completed Sample Grid Card), the group leader explains that, in each section of the card, the participant is to list some factor or quality that motivates him or her to accomplish assigned tasks competently and/or further his or her professional expertise.
3. After five minutes the trainer asks the participants to form pairs and then exchange cards with their partners. (If the group contains an uneven number, one group of three may be formed.) After reading his or her partner's card, each participant places a check mark beside each item that the partners have in common.
4. Next the partners each take back their own cards and together discuss the factors that motivate them and how, in turn, they feel they can motivate others.
5. The trainer may process the activity by having the pairs share with the entire group the listed items that they share in common and the conclusions

or insights they have reached about personal and professional motivations.

Variations
■ The trainer may have the group members use the grid format to examine barriers to effective performance. After the group members have examined motivators, the trainer gives each of them a second grid upon which they are to identify factors that inhibit job performance. The group members then compare and discuss the two grids.

■ The group leader may ask the participants to select and then record the factors that motivate them in their personal lives.

■ Prior to the exercise, the trainer may have prepared a list of motivational factors. After the participants have completed step #2 in the Trainer Administration section, the group leader tells them that they will be playing a variation of the game of Bingo. The trainer then reads the items on the list, one at a time. Each participant places a check mark by any item that matches one that the trainer reads. The winner is the first participant to match a line down, across, or diagonally. A discussion on both common and uncommon motivational factors then ensues.

Trainer's Notes

COMPLETED SAMPLE GRID CARD

Salary	Benefits	Vacation Time
Comfortable Work Environment	Job Responsibilities	Enjoyable Co-Workers
Status of Position	Power	Attention from Others

Motivators

Activity Summary

This exercise asks the participants to examine and then list the external and internal factors that motivate their actions in their personal and professional lives. This icebreaker is effective at any time during the learning program.

Training Application

Time Reference: Approximately 15 to 20 minutes.

Group Size: Best suited for a group of 10 or more participants.

Space Required: A room that has the potential for flexible seating.

Materials Needed: For each participant, a pencil and a piece of paper.

Trainer Administration

1. While distributing pencils and pieces of paper to all of the participants, the group leader explains that this exercise is designed to help them recognize and then examine the specific motivators in their personal and professional lives.

2. Next the trainer tells the group members to divide their papers into two columns. They are to title one column "Personal Life" and the other column "Professional Life".

3. Each participant is then, for each column, to list all of the relevant external and internal factors that motivate him or her to take action or to accomplish tasks. External motivational factors may be the influence of some significant other, such as a spouse or a supervisor, salary, benefits, office size, title, the specific job responsibilities the participant carries, etc. Internal motivational factors involve the participant's attitudes, values, personal goals, etc. that encourage him or her to take action or accomplish tasks. (Each factor listed should be marked as to whether it is an external or internal motivator.)

4. After five minutes, the trainer asks the group members to form pairs and to discuss their lists with their partners.

5. The group leader may process the activity through a group discussion of the more common internal and external motivations.

Variations ■ The trainer may conduct the exercise as a group activity in which the participants share professional or personal motivators. The group leader then records these motivators on a blackboard or sheet of newsprint.

■ The group leader may ask the participants to discuss the similarities and differences between the motivators that appear in their personal and professional lives.

■ The trainer may direct the participants to list their life goals. Next to each goal the group member notes the internal and/or external factors that will motivate him or her to realize that particular goal.

Trainer's Notes

_____

_____

_____

_____

_____

_____

_____

_____

Perfect Environment

This exercise challenges the participants to create ideal work environments. This icebreaker is effective at any time during the learning program.

Time Reference: Approximately 25 to 30 minutes.

Group Size: Best suited for a group of 12 or more participants.

Space Required: A room that has the potential for flexible seating.

Materials Needed: For each participant, a pencil and a piece of paper.

1. While giving each group member a pencil and a piece of paper, the trainer asks the participants to think about what they feel would be the ideal work environment.
2. The group leader then explains that each participant is to write a scenario of the circumstances that will create the perfect work environment he or she has in mind. To do this, each group member is to list on paper the specifics of the physical environment, the characteristics of the work task, the relationships among the personnel, the benefits the total work environment gives to the employee and to the company/agency/organization, and any other factors or situations that the participant feels are important to the creation of his or her ideal work environment.
3. After 10 minutes the trainer asks the participants to form work groups of four members each and to discuss their lists with their fellow work group members.
4. Then the members of each work group are to look' at their present work setting(s) and to consider those elements that they can change so that the particular work environment moves toward the ideals they have each established. Next the work group members identify the steps that can be taken to make such changes in their current work environment(s).
5. The trainer may then process the activity through a full-group discussion of how to move real work environments in the direction of the ideal.

■ Following step #4 in the Trainer Administration section, the group leader may direct the work group members to assume that they are the owners of the work environment. They then examine their ideal environments to see, in light of their position of ownership, which qualities remain on the lists, which are deleted, and which must be added.

■ The trainer may ask that the members of each work group set priorities on the items on the lists they have written. The members of each work group then attempt to reach a consensus of priorities on one list of environmental factors. Next the group leader calls the work groups together and asks them to share, and then compare and contrast, their lists.

**Trainer's
Notes**

_____

_____

_____

_____

_____

_____

_____

_____

Salesmanship

This exercise asks the participants to identify the qualities and/or facts that influence them to purchase a product and then to define the qualities of the effective salesperson. This icebreaker is effective at any time during the learning program.

Training Application

Time Reference: Approximately 15 to 20 minutes.

Group Size: Best suited for a group of 12 or more participants.

Space Required: A room that is large enough to accommodate the comfortable seating of the participants.

Materials Needed: For each participant, a pencil and a piece of paper.

Trainer Administration

1. The group leader first explains that in this exercise the participants will be identifying the qualities and/or facts that influence them to buy a particular product and then defining the qualities that are essential to effective salesmanship.

2. While distributing pencils and paper to all of the group members, the trainer tells them that they are to envision themselves as potential customers for a vacuum cleaner representative who will be trying to sell them his or her product.

3. The trainer then asks the group members to consider the following question: Assuming that they have no vacuum cleaner, what points, facts, qualities, etc. must the salesperson present to them in order to interest them in actually purchasing the item? The participants are then given three minutes to answer this question by listing the qualities/facts on their sheets of paper.

4. Next the trainer asks the group members to consider this question: What qualities and/or skills must the salesperson possess if he or she is to keep their interest and possibly sell them a vacuum cleaner? The participants are then given three minutes to answer the question by listing the qualities/skills on their pieces of paper.

5. When the participants have completed their lists, the trainer asks them to break into small discussion

groups of four to five members each. The discussion group members are first to compare and contrast their responses to the two questions. The members of each group are then to attempt to reach a consensus on the five most important product qualities and the five most important salesmanship qualities.

6. After 10 minutes the trainer reassembles the large group and asks a representative from each discussion group to report on his or her group's findings.

7. After all of the groups have presented their reports, the trainer may initiate a general discussion on the basic strategies of effective salesmanship.

Variations

■ The trainer may conduct the activity as a group exercise by posing the questions to the group as a whole and then recording the participants' responses on a blackboard or on newsprint.

■ The group leader may choose another item that is more closely related to the group members' profession(s). For example: an automobile, an insurance policy, a computer, a piece of furniture, an appliance, a piece of pipe, a beer can, etc.

Trainer's Notes

_____

_____

_____

_____

_____

_____

_____

_____

Skits

This exercise asks the participants, working in small groups, to act out stressful events and their resolutions in a humorous manner. This directed experience is best implemented after the participants have had some opportunity to engage in feedback and disclosure during the learning program.

Time Reference: Approximately 25 to 30 minutes.
Group Size: Unlimited, but best suited for a group of 30 or fewer participants.
Space Required: An unobstructed area without tables or chairs. Several small meeting rooms or areas that provide private or semiprivate interaction are also needed.
Materials Needed: None.

1. The group leader begins the exercise by telling the participants that they are going to work in groups to resolve stressful situations they encounter in their work environment(s).
2. Next the trainer asks the group members to divide into work groups of four or five participants each.
3. When the groups have formed, the trainer tells them that after they have received their instructions, they are to disperse to find rooms or areas where the members of each group can work together with some degree of privacy. The trainer then explains that each work group is to think of various stressful situations or events that occur at work. For example: deadlines that must be met, the monthly visit of a top corporate executive, a project that suddenly develops problems, a personal conflict between co-workers, etc.
4. Each work group is then to select one stressful situation that at least most of the members have experienced in some form. Next the work group members are to decide what they feel is the best solution to the particular problem or stressful situation.
5. Each work group is then to prepare a humorous skit, with practical implications, in which all of the group's members have some part in acting out the event and its resolution.

6. After explaining the exercise, the trainer tells the groups to disperse to private areas where they then plan and practice their skits.
7. After 10 minutes the trainer calls all of the work groups together and, one at a time, each group performs its skit for the entire group.
8. When all of the groups have finished their presentations, the trainer initiates a group discussion in which the participants talk over the serious implications of the skits and their relevance to the stresses inherent in work-related endeavors and, possibly, in the training program itself.

Variations
■ The trainer may conduct the exercise as a group activity in which volunteers humorously act out stressful situations selected by the entire group. The group members then brainstorm various resolutions.
■ The trainer asks each work group to act out its stressful situation and resolution in a serious manner. Other work groups then may immediately improvise alternative solutions to the issues each skit has raised.

Trainer's Notes

_____

_____

_____

_____

_____

_____

_____

_____

_____

Taking a Chance

Activity Summary

This exercise tests the willingness of the participants to take an unidentified risk. This activity is generally more effective when used in the early stage of the group's formation.

Training Application

Time Reference: Approximately 5 to 10 minutes.
Group Size: Unlimited.
Space Required: A room that is large enough to accommodate the comfortable seating of the participants.
Materials Needed: None.

Trainer Administration

1. The trainer begins the exercise by saying "I need volunteers to take part in an exercise that carries potentially very high risks for the participants. Would anyone like to volunteer?"
2. If the group members ask any questions, the trainer simply responds with "Just trust me." (Most likely, the group leader will receive few, if any, volunteers.)
3. The group leader waits for several minutes and then says, "You have just completed the exercise."
4. If any group members did volunteer, the trainer then asks these individuals to explain their reasons for offering themselves as participants in what was stated to be a high-risk activity.
5. The trainer concludes the exercise with a group discussion in which the participants examine risk taking within their professional environment, i.e., need, opportunities, barriers, consequences, etc.

Variation

■ Before the exercise the trainer may privately solicit one group member to serve as his or her confederate. The group leader begins by telling the group that the confederate is going to lead the exercise and then asks for volunteers to take part in the high-risk activity.

Trainer's Notes

_____

_____

_____

**Trainer's
Notes**
continued

_____

_____

_____

_____

_____

Three Supervisory Styles

Activity Summary   This exercise asks the participants to role play three major supervisory styles. This icebreaker is effective at any time during the learning program.

Training Application

Time Reference: Approximately 25 to 30 minutes.

Group Size: Unlimited, but best suited for a group of 10 to 20 participants.

Space Required: A room that has the potential for flexible seating.

Materials Needed: For each participant, a copy of the Incident Description Sheet (see the last page of this exercise).

Trainer Administration

1. The trainer first asks the group members to form a circular seating arrangement.

2. When the participants are seated, the group leader explains that this exercise focuses on three primary styles of supervision: the *authoritarian style*, a rigid approach characterized by the statement "You do as I say!"; the *laissez-faire style*, a loose approach in which "Whatever you want to do is fine"; and the *democratic style*, a group-oriented approach typified by "Let's talk this over."

3. Explaining that the group members will be role playing the three supervisory styles, the trainer places two chairs in the center of the circle and then gives each participant a copy of the Incident Description Sheet.

4. The group leader then solicits two volunteers to act out the first role play. The volunteers sit in the center of the circle and quickly decide who will assume the role of supervisor and who will serve as supervisee.

5. The trainer explains that, without telling the group or the "supervisee," the volunteer serving as supervisor is to choose and act out one of the three supervisory styles in his or her role play of the first situation. The volunteer serving as supervisee is to give what is her or his typical response to the chosen supervisory style.

6. At a signal from the trainer, the first role play begins. After two minutes the role play stops, and the group members attempt to identify the style

the supervisor has used. Finally, the two volunteers discuss the feelings they experienced during the role play.

7. The two volunteers then return to the circle, and two new volunteers come forward to role play the second situation from the Incident Description Sheet. Again, the supervisor is to select and act out one of the three supervisory styles.

8. The exercise continues until all five incidents have been role played and discussed.

Variations

■ The trainer may assume the role of the supervisor.

■ The group leader may whisper in the supervisor's ear the supervisory style he or she is to use in role playing the particular incident.

■ The trainer may ask that the role play for each incident be enacted twice. In the first role play, the supervisee gives his or her typical response to the supervisory style being used; in the second enactment the supervisee gives what he or she feels is the ideal reaction to the same style.

■ The group leader may request that the volunteers create their own incidents, each supervisor acting as he or she feels his or her supervisor really would react in that specific situation.

Trainer's Notes

_____

_____

_____

_____

_____

_____

_____

INCIDENT DESCRIPTION SHEET

1. The supervisee asks the supervisor for a merit increase in salary. The supervisor does not think the employee deserves a raise at this point in time.

2. The supervisor has called in the supervisee because of constant tardiness. The supervisee has an "I don't care" attitude although his/her work has been above average.

3. A supervisee comes to the supervisor reporting that other employees have been doing half-hearted work. He/she feels that the situation is getting worse and wants the supervisor to do something about it.

4. The supervisor must ask a supervisee to cancel his/her vacation plans in order to complete a job. The supervisee is aware that this job was the supervisor's responsibility and should have been completed two weeks ago.

5. Low morale has been obvious in a department for the last three months. In order to resolve the problem, the supervisor has called in what he/she considers to be the key troublemaker. The supervisee has the union backing him/her in the event that the supervisor causes any "trouble."

Time Management

Activity Summary

This exercise asks the participants to examine their use of time in their current work settings. This ice-breaker is effective at any time during the learning program.

Training Application

Time Reference: Approximately 25 to 30 minutes.
Group Size: Unlimited.
Space Required: A room that has the potential for flexible seating.
Materials Needed: For each participant, a pencil and a copy of the Time Management Sheet (see the last page of this exercise).

Trainer Administration

1. While giving each group member a pencil and a copy of the Time Management Sheet, the trainer explains that in this exercise the participants will be exploring the ways in which they use time in their present professional setting(s).

2. The group leader then asks the participants to fill out their sheets, the trainer should emphasize that the group members need to be as honest as possible in assessing the amount of time they spend on each indicated item.

3. When all of the group members have finished this task, the trainer requests that they pair off and then spend 10 minutes discussing their responses with their partners. During this time the partners should also discuss time priorities, barriers to time management, ways to maximize the effective use of time, time versus productivity, etc.

4. When the allotted time has elapsed, the trainer asks the partners to report on their discussions of the effective and ineffective uses of time.

5. After all of the pairs have reported their thoughts and reactions, the group leader may wish to lead a general discussion on how the participants can increase their effective use of time in their present work settings.

Variations

■ The trainer may ask each pair to formulate *specific* guidelines for effective time management. The partners then share their guidelines with the entire group.

■ The group leader may request that, before filling out the Time Management Sheet, the participants list their daily work-related activities and then set priorities on these tasks. After completing the Time Management Sheet, the participants then compare and contrast their tasks and current time allotments.

Trainer's Notes

_____

_____

_____

_____

_____

_____

_____

_____

TIME MANAGEMENT SHEET

1. I spend _____ minutes a day getting ready to actually work.

2. I spend _____ minutes a day thinking productively.

3. I spend _____ minutes a day reading reports.

4. I spend _____ minutes a day filling out paperwork.

5. I spend _____ minutes a day in nonproductive daydreaming.

6. I spend _____ minutes a day in nonwork-related conversations.

7. I spend _____ minutes a day in work-related conversations.

8. I spend _____ minutes a day trying to organize my day.

9. I spend _____ minutes a day eating.

10. I spend _____ minutes a day exercising or relaxing.

11. I spend _____ minutes a day on unnecessary interruptions.

12. I spend _____ minutes a day on specific work-related tasks.

Typical Workday

Activity Summary

This exercise asks the participants to examine the stresses that are part of their daily work routines. This icebreaker is effective at any time during the learning program.

Training Application

Time Reference: Approximately 30 minutes.
Group Size: Unlimited.
Space Required: A room that is large enough to accommodate the comfortable seating of the participants.
Materials Needed: For each participant, a pencil and a piece of paper; for the trainer, the Sample Stresses and Tasks Sheet (see the last page of this exercise).

Trainer Administration

1. The group leader tells the participants that in this exercise they will be asked to consider the various stress factors that affect their daily lives.
2. While giving each participant a pencil and a piece of paper, the trainer directs the group members to think of the stressful situations they encounter during a typical workday and then any ways in which they can reduce these stresses by more effectively managing their time, routines, daily responsibilities, etc.
3. After several minutes the group leader asks that each participant list, in a column running down the left side of his or her paper, the occurrences or situations that cause stress for him or her during a typical workday.
4. Then, in a column running down the right side of the paper, each group member is to list, in order of priority, the tasks he or she needs to accomplish during a normal workday.
5. When they have completed their lists, the participants are to draw lines between the two columns, connecting stresses and tasks that seem to have some relationship (see the Sample Stresses and Tasks Sheet).
6. The trainer then asks the group members to pair off and to discuss their typical days with their partners. Next the partners are to formulate plans for

disconnecting the lines on their sheets. For example: requesting a hold on phone calls for the time required to total daily receipts (see Sample Stresses and Tasks Sheet for more examples).

7. After 10 minutes the group leader then calls the participants together and concludes the exercise with a full-group discussion in which the participants brainstorm general guidelines for recognizing and then alleviating stress in their work environments.

Variation

■ The trainer may have the participants, working individually, devise and list their own solutions to stressful connections. Then in a group discussion the participants share their strategies and focus on common stressful situations and possible solutions to them.

Trainer's Notes

_____

_____

_____

_____

_____

_____

_____

_____

SAMPLE STRESSES AND TASKS SHEET

Stress-Producing Factors

Daily Tasks (in priority)

Lack of privacy

Unrealistic deadlines on paperwork

Coping with my supervisor

Boredom with the nature of the work

Constant interruptions

Inadequate office space

Inability to get clear-cut answers to simple questions

Accountability forms that are unnecessary

Putting up with constant office gossip

Four interviews daily

Employee performance reports

Filing personnel data

Gathering management information forms

Setting times for new interviews

Returning phone calls concerning employment inquiries

Organizing material for the yearly report